VISION

how brain science
and hunting goblins
will help you see yourself
and your future
with **clarity**

Jeremy DeRuiter

Published by Grumblebub Ventures, LLC

Special pricing is available for bulk purchases of this book for use in education or employee support programs.

Printed in the United States
ISBN 979-8-218-52141-7

Design by Jeremy DeRuiter
Edited by Nicholle Robertson

www.grumblebub.com

This is book is dedicated to my parents.
I am the clay you shaped, the book you wrote.
I am myself, but you showed me the way.

Contents

Foreword IX

Preface XIII

The Back Seat of Life 1

My Script Made Me Do It 3

Inertia, Our Brains, and Saber-toothed Tigers 8

Waking Up 10

Get in Motion: Scripts and Inertia 11

What Makes You Tick? 13

Your Subconscious 19

The New Kid 20

The Know-it-All 22

The Coach 23

Get in Motion: Your Subconscious and Waking Up 26

Our "Stories" 27

The Dreaded "K." 27

The Never-Ending Novel 29

Weighed Down By Our Past 30

The Locker Room Trap 32

Get in Motion: Rewriting Your Stories 35

What a Worldview 37

We're All the Hero of Our Own Story 37

"A-Hole" to "Hospital" 39

An Honest Perspective 42

Get in Motion: Working with Perspective 45

THE NASTY BITS BENEATH THE SURFACE **49**
Alright, Judgy McJudgerton 50
A Tragic Expression 51
Your Ugly Little Goblin 54
Get in Motion: Find Your Goblin(s) 58

ENERGY **61**
Four Types of Energy 63
Figuring Out My Funk 64
It's Not All Equal 67
The Milksteamer's Moody Mirror 69
The Introvert at the 600-Person Party 73
Get in Motion: Understanding Your Energy 77

How's Your Vision? **79**

WAYS OF BEING **83**
Your Presets 84
How Can I Be for You Today? 86
Patrick, My Emotional Role Model 88
Get in Motion: Identifying Your Ways of Being 89

HOW DO I BE ME? **91**
It Takes a Village (of Nerds): Jeremy Finds a Place to Belong 92
The Lessons My Classes Taught Me About Me 95
You in All of Your Glorious You-ness 97
P.S. Opinions Are Like...You Know 101
Get in Motion: Showing Up as Your Full True Self 102

SELF-PERCEPTION IS NOT REALITY **105**
You Are NOT Here 107

We Take What We Know for Granted 109
The Person in the Mirror is Your Friend—Act Accordingly 112
Our Self-Perception Isn't Rooted in Objective Reality 113
Get in Motion: Self-Perception and Seeing Yourself Clearly 114

Stop Hitting Yourself! **117**
Me, Myself, and My Inner Bully 118
Cozy Up to the Squirm 120
Self-Deprecating Humor 123
Accepting Compliments 126
Get in Motion: You and Your Self-Talk and Self-Love 129

Can You See Where You're Going? **131**

Let's Dream a Little Dream, Shall We? **133**
How I Visioned My Way into a Demotion 135
The Power of Sharing 139
Forecasting and the Fog 142
Dashboard of Dreams 145
Get in Motion: Visioning 149

The Power of Your Mind **151**
Placebos, Nocebos, and Other Brain Trickery 151
Meditation is a Super Power 154
Visualizing Like a Champ 157
The Air Traffic Controller in Your Brain 159
Rehearsals for Your Dream Life 161
Get in Motion: Start Your Vision Board 164

How Do You Want to Be? **167**
Clarity from Common Language 168

An Achiever Wrestles with Himself at the Riverside 170
Best Self 173
Worst Self 177
The Bossy Finger 180
Get in Motion: How Do You Want to Be? 183

What Do You Want to Do? 185
The Costs of Changing Direction 187
When Your Money is Your Life 191
You Are Here 197
A 30,000 Foot View of Your Life 198
A Moonshot in the Rough 200
Get in Motion: Your Eulogy and Moonshot 203

Bleary-Eyed and Stumbling Forth 205
Acknowledgements 209
Notes 212
Index 215
Also by Jeremy DeRuiter 220

Foreword

Most certainly I will get to the project at hand, this book, and extol the work for what it is, a look inside the inner sanctum of a human being I respect and who is on their life's quest, a journey deep into their own mind and soul. But first, I must talk about Jeremy. Somebody I have known over 20 years, who I would consider a close friend. The kind I drink beer and golf with? No. Friend, as in somebody I could call any minute, of any day and know he would be there for me? Yes. One of those rare people who you know has your back no matter the circumstances.

Jeremy has always been a luminary. Somebody I run my thinking past to check my north. Sometimes done for real in full reality but most often through cosmic means, in my own brain and spirit. Something akin to, "What would Jeremy think?" "What would Jeremy do?" Very few people garner this status in the world. Who are your cosmic leaders? List is short, eh?

Why is Jeremy this for me? Well in short, after reading this book, I think you will understand. Jeremy is a good human being. He is a thinker. He is a doer. Jeremy is fun to be around. Most importantly he cares deeply, and his intentions are aligned with supporting you, me, anyone he connects with in building their own uniqueness, their own life that they love.

My endorsement of the author, complete. Now to this project, Jeremy's book, Vision.

Self-help, self-improvement, personal development texts are written by people who are smarter and wiser than you. The author espousing theory based on their experience in life, in the world. For me, most fall short as we are not allowed inside the inner sanctum of the author. We are getting the shimmering and polished version of the story.

But, those who are truly great at writing in this genre, writing this content are those who are not afraid to open up the kimono and let the reader see and feel what is going on within the inner recesses of the soul when traversing this work on themself. People love Brenè Brown because she gives you true stories, warts and all. The real stuff, so much so at times you can't believe the stories she is telling you.

Jeremy does this as well in his book. You get to see the underbelly of JD, the warts and all. For example, his depiction of his morning routine, shuffling to the bathroom & conversations with the guy in the mirror, brings you into the soul of Jeremy DeRuiter as well as I have seen an author open up and invite the reader into the inner sanctum ever. The conversations he is having with himself are the real thing. This makes Jeremy real, Jeremy's work powerful.

Additionally, this is a quest by a guy that could be you or me, because Jeremy is you or me. It feels different and better than so many other self-help books because while most are written by world-class performers, or professors at Harvard, or CEOs of Fortune 500 companies and are interesting and inspiring, they're just not relatable. Jeremy brilliantly uses everyday moments we all live but never articulate, making this book feel like a depiction of our own lives. From doing errands with Dad as a young boy, to bullying in middle school, to performance in college, to his first date with Megan, to analysis of his mindset commuting, etc. We get to see and feel real life.

His depictions of himself are vivid and sparkling. For example, his description of himself as a "people-pleasing-question-answering-heat-seeking-missile of a man," made me laugh out loud. Or, when he invites you to "come along on a journey into my pettiness." These are the moments that make the book real and poignant. Jeremy invites you into the real time video playing in his head as he ruminates and explores his experience in the world. This is a lovely, entertaining and insightful experience.

Finally, as entertaining, engaging and funny as this book is, the content and the message are powerful. Jeremy explores the power of visioning, a subject Jeremy and I have connected on together for many years. He makes visioning practical and applies it within everyday life. He shows how the act of writing down our vision primes our minds for making our dreams come true—it might feel like magic, but there's brain science at work. Meanwhile, the Goblin metaphor works perfectly and I appreciated the imagery of turning my brain into an out of control Goblin. Funny, a little scary, and useful.

I could go on and on but suffice it to say I am proud of Jeremy and I love what he has put together here in Vision.

With all my heart I want to express gratitude to Jeremy for writing this book and I am endorsing it fully as I think everyone can learn from Jeremy's ability to articulate the lessons he has learned from his experience.

Godspeed!
Mike

Michael J. McFall
Ann Arbor, MI
January 2025

Preface

Hey there. I'm glad you're here.

Vision is a book that only I could have written.

It's not a boast. It's just an affirmation that what you're about to read is a distillation of some of the most important things I've learned along the way from the people around me and in some cases from the books I've read. It's a piece of my life and thoughts, captured as best as I was able.

Because it's me, you'll find that it's properly nerdy, personable, heartfelt, funny, vulnerable, and well-intentioned.

I wrote it across 2022 and 2023, followed by six months of working on finding a literary agent. One of them was kind enough to send me feedback suggesting that I self-publish and share it first within the world of BIGGBY COFFEE. Since then, I've learned what I needed to in order to arrive at this moment, as you read these words.

I'm not an influencer. I'm not a CEO. I don't have a PhD. I don't have the kind of "platform" that agents or publishers are willing to take a risk on.

But I might know a few things that will help you to build a life you love. And if that proves true, my time will have been well spent.

My time with BIGGBY has shaped who I am and I'm so grateful for the hundreds of relationships I've built with members of our community. You've had a profound impact on my life. I hope this book pays forward your investment in me.

With love,
Jeremy

Toddler Jeremy at typewriter

Chapter One

The Back Seat of Life

I love books. I have always loved books.

On Saturday mornings, Dad would have my brother and me draw folded-up pieces of paper from a bowl to determine which bits of fun we'd be sprinkling into the monotony of Dad's boring errands (Picture us whining: "Ugh...not Fruit Basket Flowerland again...it's the wooooooooorst, Dad!")

Putt Putt Golf and the Fun Factory arcade were highly prized picks—and exceedingly rare.

While some kids may have regarded drawing "Library" or "Used book store" as barely better than "Fruit Basket" from the bowl, those were still winners in my...book! The library promised the opportunity to come home with a whole stack of books—so many choices, such variety, my blue eyes wide and excited behind my oversized eighties-kid glasses. The used bookstore meant creaky wood floors and the intoxicating mustiness of books passed from hand to hand, bookshelf to bookshelf, across generations, and me heavy with the responsibility of choosing the one book I would buy that day and add to my growing collection in our bedroom.

Whether on those errands, or on a road trip up north to Mackinac Island, I guarantee you would have found me in the back seat, nose buried in one of those books.

Upon earning my driver's license, I discovered that I didn't know how to navigate my own town. I never paid any attention. Up until that point I was simply carried along from place to place, never giving any notice to my surroundings.

Many of us let our lives pass by in much the same way. We're along for the ride, head down, taken from one stop to the next.

Here's what it might look like: Wake up, clean up, go to work, get home, binge a Netflix series, go to sleep. Wake up the next day, clean up, go to work, get home, scroll through social media, go to sleep. Wake up the next day, clean up, go to work, and so on. Day after day. Week after week. Month after month. Years pass, punctuated here and there by new and exciting things, but generally, the same ol' same ol' routine carries us along.

This is the momentum of life.

We get swept away by the momentum of life. Hurtling forward from one day to the next month to the next year!

Why do we do the things we do?
The answer: momentum.

No particular choices being made, just being carried along in the back seat of our own lives.

Does that sound familiar to you?

You may be happy and feel complete in life, being carried along in the way I described. Which is awesome. I've spent most of my life that way. I had a vague sense of direction and I was happy enough. But I was also missing out.

Maybe you sense something is missing. Is there something more? If only you knew what it was and how to get there.

There's good news: It doesn't take much effort to climb from the back seat and get behind the wheel to regain control over where you're going in life.

It does require work, but I promise from experience that it's the kind of work where you'll see the benefits immediately.

You ready?

My Script Made Me Do It

Many of us are following scripts that were written for us.

For most of us, our parents did the writing, with our extended family and institutions like school and church stepping in to lend a hand. Our script outlines how the world works. It establishes good and bad. There are expectations for us in the script, sometimes right there in the text, sometimes between the lines.

Here's a small and silly example...I grew up believing there was a jolly old fat man in a red outfit who came down our chimney, ate some cookies, drank some milk, grabbed carrots for his reindeer sidekicks, and dropped off a load of presents for me and my brother because we'd been good boys. I was in first grade when a kid on the school bus told me that Santa wasn't real.

That's how scripts work. We follow along, assuming it's how the world works.

I wouldn't have known this word at the time but looking back: the kid was SMUG. Other kids nearby were nodding along, with looks in their eyes that would suggest that they were having empathetic flashbacks to their own moment of revelation. And POOF! My little six-year-old worldview fractured. It was a lie. The smug third grader said so. I don't remember the reckoning that happened when I got home, but there was no going back.

Right up until the point where something or somebody jars us from our perspective, creating an opportunity to examine that script and question what's true versus what might be just one version of the truth.

Now Santa is the rare example where parents very knowingly lie to their children, setting them up for disappointment.

Here's a less-silly bit of scripting my parents wrote for me (without intending to): I will get married, as early as 21-years-old and as late as 25-years-old and have children, preferably two of them. That process will be underway before I hit 30.

I remember bumping against that script psychologically as I entered my mid-twenties. My parents married when Mom was 21 and Dad was 25. I'd had a couple serious girlfriends along the way, but when I turned 25, I had very few prospects.

I never realized how difficult it was going to become to meet women once I moved out of the dorm and more so once I left college. Gone were the days of people living up and down the hall from me or having friends living a few blocks away in every direction. Socializing now required making plans and aligning schedules in a way I hadn't done before. Recognizing the issue at hand, I signed up for the neolithic version of some online dating site and went on a couple dates. Nothing worked.

And oooooh did I feel it. Today, happily married and in my forties, it's funny looking back at my 24-year-old self. Poor kid. At 24, I. Was. In. My. Feelings. I know this because my playlists of the day were consumed with very earnest and very sad music.

Here's what I didn't recognize back then: I felt like a failure. Mom and Dad were MARRIED at this point. Sure, they ended up divorced, but hey, try telling my 24-year-old brain that. My subconscious was ringing the alarm bells, and even louder as one by one, four of my close friends married. Meanwhile, I was single, single, single.

There was good news on my horizon, I just didn't know it. A few months later, I went out on my first date with Megan.

We met in college. She sang in Ladies First, an a capella group at Michigan State. She was (and remains) beautiful and talented. She came into my orbit thanks to my roommate, Nathan, who sang a cappella in the Spartan Dischords. We met at a house party in 2000. She claims I ignored her. Might have been true, but it was justified—I was in a relationship at the time, close to ending, as it would turn out.

A few years later, deep into the single, single, single era, there was Megan, at a Halloween party. Full disclosure: I'm a disappointing Halloween party guest. It was true then and it's true today because I hate wasting money and time to come up with a costume that I wear the one night.

That night I was wearing a costume cobbled together hastily from my closet. The sort of costume that needs to be explained. At some point in the evening, I explained my "costume" to Megan, and she gave me the well-deserved "uuuuhhh huhhh" reaction. She ignored me the rest of the night. Years later she explained that she gave me the cold shoulder due to the discomfort of an ex-boyfriend also being at the party, not because of my lame Halloween costume.

And yet, in January of 2005, over at Nathan's house for dinner, he told me Megan was single AND she thought I was cute. WHAT'S HER NUMBER? I was so eager it's amazing that I didn't call her from the dinner table.

I remember her walking up to my car for our first date. So, so, beautiful. I was a raw nerve. We went to a Spanish restaurant on the recommendation of my brother. Everything was fantastic. She was a high school English teacher, and me an English major, and she was so funny. We hit it off, chatting and laughing, small plate after small plate, wine, mojitos, and the much-anticipated paella.

I'd later learn how far outside her comfort zone Megan went with me that evening (I just snorted out loud as I typed that last sentence). A Sunday night date? For a teacher?! Terrible choice. An awesome Spanish-themed restaurant with an adventurous menu? Yeah, turns out she's a picky eater. But at least there's wine! She likes wine just fine, thank you, but was likely feeeeeeling it heading into her second glass! And a spicy paella for the main course? Woof. Wrong on three different levels.

And yet. It didn't matter. It was Megan and me. And we are GREAT together. All the chemistry you could ever hope for.

We got serious quickly and started tossing around marriage within a few months of that first date. Somehow, we just knew we were right for each other.

Or was it our scripts?

I'd like to think it was just that magic spark between us, but who knows? I share more than a few traits with her father, and she is every bit as smart and funny as my mother.

Our scripts...the things that just feel right in life...are powerful. We can follow them for years without realizing their influence. They can be destructive and they can be productive. They can be limiting or empowering. They can help you fall in love.

I started shopping for a ring a year later and proposed over a candlelit dinner that I prepared. We said "I do" in 2007 with just about every person in the world who loved us watching. My face hurt from smiling.

My next script-related revelation thundered through my life when I turned 29. Megan and I had been married for just over a year. Work had me traveling frequently, which added stress, but on the

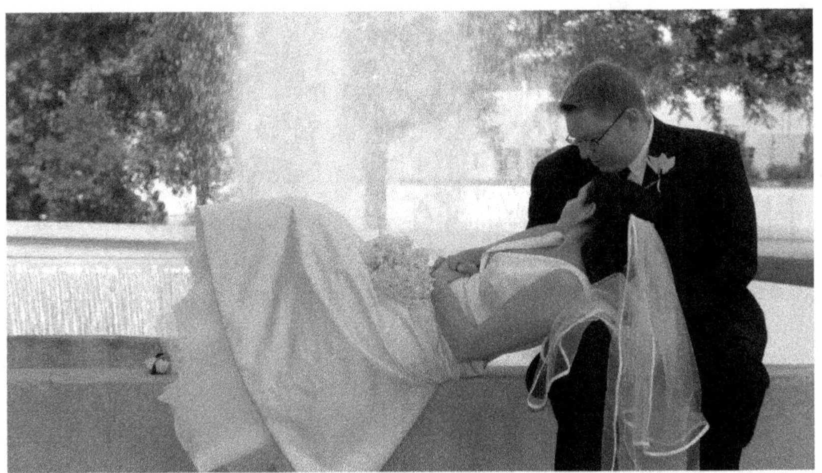

Megan, and me all gaga about her, as it ever has been

whole, things were really good. We talked about getting a dog, and while we weren't ready for kids, we knew that was THE PLAN. Twenty-nine came and went, and we still weren't interested in "pulling the goalie."

But I was supposed to start having kids by now, wasn't I? My script was trying to reassert itself, applying pressure to the back of my brain.

Megan and I checked in periodically: "You want kids yet?" "No, I'm good, you?" "Nope, I'm good." Meanwhile, our friends were on the Procreation Wagon. Good grief, my best friend was off to the races—four kids in three years!

Our parents needled, "When will you give us grandkids?" We dragged our feet. It wasn't a "no," it was a "not now."

Megan and I stumbled into a crucial realization: The reason we wanted to have kids was to give our parents grandchildren. It was the script. Again. This is what is expected of us. This is what we're supposed to do. This notion was the wake-up call we needed. It helped us see our script. Once we actually thought about what we wanted, rather than what we thought we should want, it made all the difference.

We felt no need to become parents.

Scripts are powerful, especially when they remain unexamined. They can have positive or negative effects on our life, subtly steering our decision-making and framing our outlook on the world around us.

But it's more than just scripts. Scripts set the direction and create the momentum. Inertia, however, is what keeps us headed that way, our heads down, getting carried along, doing the same thing we did yesterday, over and over again.

Inertia, Our Brains, and Saber-toothed Tigers

There's brain science at play. Our brains burn gobs of energy when we think hard. The part responsible for our conscious thought, the prefrontal cortex, is super-inefficient, energy-wise, so when we summon our willpower repeatedly to get through the day (skipping the donuts, reining in the impulse to get snippy with a coworker, resisting the beckoning call of social media while in a boring meeting, etc.), by the time we reach the end of it, our willpower is s-p-e-n-t. How many pizzas and happy meals have been sold based on this? (Answer: a bazillion...'I don't want to think, and I don't want to slow down, but I need to feed myself and these kids, so...')

This is what makes habits powerful. When you're new to a task, you just rip through brain energy, with your "associative loop" running the show. After enough repetitions, your associative loop hands over the keys to a different part of your brain, the sensorimotor loop, a tightfisted caretaker of brain energy.

It's like this: While driving, have you ever snapped back to being fully present to realize that you don't know where you are? Maybe you missed your exit or realized you are miles further into your trip than expected because you weren't really paying attention. Scary, no? Well, that, friend, is the power of habit at work.

I picture our ancient ancestors picking berries while consciously attuning every other sense to scan for saber-toothed tigers. Those who were especially efficient at that bit of neural multi-tasking won the Darwinian competition. And today, as the beneficiary of that evolutionary inheritance, I never need to think about brushing my teeth in the morning. And I don't make a conscious decision to check my phone when I'm bored or notice that I'm 10 minutes into scrolling when I should have been reading my book. Our brains have become hyper-efficient at transforming repeated behaviors into thoughtless habits that propel us through our day.

Habit and diminished willpower do a lot to keep us doing the easy, predictable thing from one moment to the next.

I know many people who have demanding jobs that occupy 40-plus hours of their attention each week who go home to equally demanding home lives. Just like a phone where the battery is past its prime, some of these folks have to put themselves into power saver mode each day to try to make it to Friday. They avoid anything that might present an additional strain on their time, emotions, or energy. They take the same route to work, listening to the same music, that they did yesterday. They get takeout on the way home and attend to their kids or other obligations and in the margins where they have free moments they rewatch shows they've seen many times before. Wake up the next day and wash, rinse, repeat. They know they're not living fully. They experience guilt and shame over it. But they feel powerless to change and they get swept away, day to month to year by the Momentum of Life.

Listen: It's okay. You can still be a relatively happy drained battery. And believe me, I'm fully on board with turning to some tasty takeout and diving deep into a multi-season weekend-long binge. Totally fun. Totally fine. But maybe, just maybe, there's more that's available if we could just wake up.

And guess what? Waking up is just the start. It can get fun, quick. You can get in the driver's seat. You get to choose where you go. You get to choose the stops along the way. It will be incredible. It's also going to take some work, friend.

But if you're reading this, I suspect you're ready to roll.

Let's go!

Waking Up

This becomes a little bit of a Choose Your Adventure at this point. I could suggest that there's just one way, just one path, to taking control of your life, but life is way too squiggly to declare a single way to do things. Instead, I'm going to lay out the places you're going to have to go (or perhaps revisit) in order to get moving.

Pretty good bet that you already have a handle on some of these areas, and that's great.

- **Figure out what makes you tick (Chapters 2-6):** This is like noticing your nose...it's always there, always in your field of view, but you just don't give it any attention. This is where you'll get clear that the way you are built and how you perceive the world is not the Truth or Right or Wrong, but just...the way you see it. Once you can notice the filter you've been viewing life through, you can take ownership over your perspective and use it to your advantage.

- **Cultivate an empowering self-image (Chapters 7-10):** Along the way to figuring out what makes you tick, you'll likely realize that you also have a warped self-image. Perhaps you engage in toxic self-talk, saying to yourself either aloud or in your head "you idiot" after making a mistake, or "ugh, you're disgusting" when you look in the mirror in the morning. That sort of behavior is holding you back whether you know it or not. The good news: once you become conscious of all that crud, you can replace it with empowering habits.

- **Use visioning to create a path (Chapters 11-14):** Invest time dreaming about who you want to be and what you want to do with your life and then get it down on paper. If you want to live intentionally and not just be swept along following your script or doing what's easiest, you need to write your own story so you can start living it!

That's the adventure that lies before us. I'm going to push you to get moving. Gently. Firmly. Lovingly. Pushing. The folks at the BIGGBY COFFEE Home Office whom I've coached will be nodding right about now. They'll recognize my preference for action. And there's good reason for that: good ideas won't change your life, won't help others, and won't make the world a better place. Acting on good ideas just might. So let's get moving!

Get in Motion: Scripts and Inertia

I wonder if you've already started this activity in the back of your mind. This is about becoming conscious of the scripts that you may have been following your entire life. This is about waking up. About becoming present to the forces that have swept you along, maybe without you noticing. This is about giving you a chance to be in the driver's seat!

Two options: Get ready to write or, if writing feels like it would be a drag, grab someone in your life and discuss. Just reading these prompts won't do anything for you, sorry. You need to engage. Writing down your thoughts or talking through them with someone close to you will help you to have powerful takeaways and get into action. Just thinking about them means you added a few more thoughts to the thousands you already had today. So, get going and get these thoughts out of your head and into the world!

1. How are you—your character and behaviors—similar to your parents?
2. How have your life choices so far mirrored your parents?
3. How have your life choices so far not mirrored your parents? Do you or they have feelings about this?
4. In your day-to-day life, where are you choosing to do the "easy" thing rather than what you feel you would be better off doing?
5. Based on the above, is there anything you want to change about how you're going through life?
6. If you identified anything for #5, pick one that feels particularly important or exciting to consider. What would be a small step you could take today or tomorrow that would move you a little further toward that goal?
7. Now put something on your calendar or set an alarm on your phone to make sure that you won't forget. I want you to get a win here.

Section One

What Makes You Tick?

Over the last seven years, I think this has been the most valuable work that I've done—learning what makes me tick. It created a huge opportunity for me to grow. And it all started with making the transition from scoffing at self-help books to reading a couple and realizing that I had it all wrong. Working on improving myself has become a wildly productive hobby, opening all kinds of new doors for me. Not the least of which is coming full circle to the point where I wanted to share some of the things I've learned by writing my own self-helpy-type book.

I'll forever be grateful to Bob Fish and Mike McFall, CEOs and co-Founders of BIGGBY® COFFEE and my long-time bosses for bringing these kinds of self-reflective practices into our workplace. The first big a-ha moment happened on a chilly April morning out in the woods.

Bob and Mike (BaM, as they're affectionately known within the world of BIGGBY) had gotten it into mind that we should find a way to bring select franchise owners together to form self-sufficient support groups—we call them Leadership Forums.

Being a business owner can be lonely, especially if you don't have a business partner. Spouses, if not fully involved, cannot completely understand the challenges and their fears. But if we could create a structure that makes it safe for franchise owners to be open about their struggles, they could support each other with empathy and ideas for overcoming their business and home life challenges. They'd have the opportunity to become better leaders, improve their businesses and further their own personal growth.

But how do we launch one of these Forums?

Well, it starts out in the woods. Mike knew a company, Crux Move Consulting, out of Kalamazoo, MI, that wanted to help us kick-start a trusting environment. BaM decided that we would test this new process ourselves before inviting our franchisees. So, on a cold April morning, BaM, me, and my Operations team leaders—Stephanie, Brie, Laura, Alisha, and Kelli—set out for the training site.

It wasn't long before we were on our feet, shuffling a bit to keep warm, as Michael and Jim, our Crux Move facilitators, laid out two ropes in a big V shape on the ground. They walked us through a 45-minute exercise, where they introduced us to the concept of work styles and had us self-evaluate what styles we each possessed.

The first work style paring was introvert and extrovert. "What do you think of when you hear introvert and extrovert?" Michael asked us.

"Being social or awkward at a party," one of us ventured.

Michael affirmed the answer and went on to explain that's not what we're talking about. Instead, we're talking about a work style that hinges upon how we gather and process information when we set about a task.

So, Jim (a classic introvert) and Michael (a classic extrovert) illustrated the idea using an example of what this looks like if each style had to assemble a bicycle, new out of the box.

"If you're on this far end of the spectrum," Michael said, pointing to the top-right tip of the big V shape he was standing next to "this means that, as an extreme extrovert, you toss the instruction book aside and immediately start figuring out how each piece connects to each piece on your own, as you go."

"Whereas if you're a full-on introvert, over here by me," Jim said, "You start by reading through the instructions, getting all of the parts organized and the necessary tools together, and begin assembly at step one."

Michael, poking fun, said, "Yeah, you might even make some corrections in the instruction manual so that you can let the company know about their mistakes after you're done."

They described how people with an extroverted work style gather information by doing. They see mistakes as a necessary part of learning and, therefore, progress. Introverts, however, gather information first and then they go into action. They need to feel sufficiently prepared with all the necessary inputs to know how to succeed before starting because they tend to view mistakes as embarrassing, maybe even shameful.

We learned that introverts are likely to ask a lot of questions at the beginning of a new experience and will be careful with their words, editing in their head before speaking (and depending on how extreme an introvert, perhaps re-editing the re-edits of their edits). Contrasted with extroverts, who are often just as surprised by what comes out of their mouth as you might be. They act first and ask questions later.

They asked us to place ourselves along the V shape according to where we are on the spectrum, including if we felt that we were equally extroverted and introverted, to place ourselves at the base of the V.

We looked around at where people landed and things started to make A. Lot. More. Sense.

I'm rather introverted. Likely to rely on the instructions? Check. Ask lots of questions first? You bet. Run a filter in my head before speaking? Yes, yep, for sure, that too.

And the people who frustrated me most often? Standing opposite of me, over on the fairly-extremely-extroverted side of the V.

Mackey Forum launch, 2018

Then Jim and Michael gave us the gift of asking the extroverts what it was about the introverted style they appreciate, and then asked us introverts what we do that might frustrate the extroverts. Then, after some discussion, they asked the same questions in reverse.

It became clear that what we considered flaws in our opposites weren't flaws at all. Just a completely different and totally valid way of doing things. It became clear that if we could appreciate each other's work styles as strengths to rely on, combined with self-awareness about our own styles, needs, motivators, and stressors, we can become a much stronger team.

That was one part of our first exercise, among many facilitated by Michael and Jim that day. By the end of it, we were seeing each other so much more clearly than we ever had before.

It was a powerful experience. It sounds dramatic, but it helped me to see the world with new eyes. I was able to extend grace to others in a way that just never occurred to me before. My peers went from being wrong to wonderfully different.

Don't misunderstand. I still, to this day regress to my old way of thinking, deep in a work style blind spot, mired in judgment for the way someone else is working through a problem. Then one of my beautiful, wonderful, brilliant teammates asks just the right question about what my face is doing and poof! I'm back. Judgment gone. Uptightness gone. Just the latest lesson in understanding what makes me—and the people around me—tick.

So yeah. You and I are going to be getting into it, just as if we were out in the woods on a chilly spring morning in Michigan. Make sure you wear warm waterproof footwear with wool socks, okay?

VISION

Chapter Two

Your Subconscious

It's not long after birth that babies begin to absorb lessons from the world around them. We observe some of this as it happens, particularly around the time they go from "goo goo ga ga" to "mama" and "dada." They're not just learning to form the sounds, they're formulating meaning from everything around them.

Our brains were built from the very beginning to make meaning from the inputs around us. At any given moment, our brains are being flooded with sensory input. If you actually had to pay attention to all of that and make decisions from millisecond to millisecond, you'd be fried in an instant.

Thankfully, we don't have to pay attention to every detail. For better and for worse, our brains filter all of that reality, organize it into something meaningful, and prioritize it, too.

Our subconscious has coded the world around us into patterns (or schemas or maps or models; whatever you want to call it, there's some A-plus organizing happening behind the scenes). When those patterns get disturbed, it jars us back to conscious thought.

So we rely on it, but we surely suffer for our subconscious, too.

It's always been there, picking up and recording experiences that it attaches meaning to, making patterns, drawing maps, and, let's just say, writing scripts. Let's look at a script that I wrote for myself as a school kid that I didn't dig up until I was in my 30s.

The New Kid

As a young manager at BIGGBY, I suffered some painful lessons owing to things my subconscious had picked up when I was a school kid.

I owe my friend and colleague, Tony, for helping me. Actually, he was kinda' the loose tooth in the story because he was the one calling attention to the trouble I was making. Bless him for it. He saw me more clearly than I saw myself.

Here's the behavior he called out: in meetings, I had a habit of answering questions directed at others in the room. Things that had nothing to do with me but I knew the answer, so I'd butt in and steal the other person's thunder. I'm amazed I lived to see the age of 30 acting that way.

If you were the person I was speaking over, what would you think? That I'm an A-hole, or a know-it-all, or attention-seeking, or that I didn't trust them to answer correctly, or perhaps all of the above. Rightfully so!

Here's what was going on, and a reminder: I was 100% unaware of this for years. It took a lot of conversation and reflection to figure out where that impulse came from. The answer? Middle school.

I was good at school. Good at following rules. Paying attention. A curious mind, ready to learn.

My parents divorced when I was in second grade, but that didn't affect my performance at school.

The summer after fifth grade, my mom married, and my brother and I moved from a suburban school system to the country. Had we stayed in Kentwood, my graduating class would have been close to 700 students. In Delton, 115. It was a small town.

I was the new kid in a school district where many of my classmates' parents, aunts, uncles, and cousins had also attended. Where teachers would know a little about some of their students based on their last name.

I stuck out like a sore thumb, especially because Mom and I missed the memo on the dress code. I showed up for my first day at the new school wearing the-very-fashionable-at-the-time combination of black bicycle shorts, a neon green tank top, and a neon pink bicycle hat, with the brim, of course, flipped up in order to achieve maximum coolness. That was the last day in my life where I was on top of a fashion trend. I got in trouble with the vice principal because of my outfit. That's how far this sore thumb was sticking out.

I imagine a lot of people who moved around while growing up would agree that being the new kid is tough. I went from having a wide circle of friends and lots of neighborhood kids to play with to just me and my younger brother Jonathan, living in the middle of nowhere. The nearest kids that were my age were a mile away, contrasted with our old house where I had a friend living two doors to the right, two doors to the left, directly behind us, and kitty-corner. This was pre-internet, so no texting, social media, or online gaming to help stay in touch after I moved. I was rebuilding my social life from a full reset.

The one thing that remained consistent at school was teachers in charge at the front of the classroom. While the playground and lunchroom were unstructured Darwinian social experiments, in class I knew the rules and what was valued: having the right answer. Having the right answer was met with approval by the teacher. Having the right answers on tests led to good grades. Good grades were what my parents expected and also what I was rewarded for...my grandma would pay $5 for each A on my report card.

I was absolutely that stereotypical kid whose hand shot up when the teacher asked a question. I didn't sit at the front of the class, though. Just saying.

I had that trait before we moved, but it cemented into place in the new school. The classroom was a safe space. So imagine after years of school and hundreds—if not thousands—of opportunities to answer questions, how ingrained that habit was.

The Know-it-All

Flash forward. The context has shifted, but the structure is similar. Rather than having a teacher and class of kids, there's a boss and a bunch of coworkers in a meeting. Right answers, or perhaps more frequently, good ideas, are rewarded. Being an idea guy and a problem solver was a way to earn recognition.

It's a strength of mine—to be quick on my feet inside conversation, grappling with complexity, and looking for connections and solutions. And like any strength, it can be overused.

When I would go overboard, stepping on toes and sucking up all the air in the room, I felt like I was killing it. It was like scratching a mosquito bite until it bleeds...it felt too good to realize I was doing damage.

I kept up that behavior for years. It's embarrassing to consider.

As the years progressed, I continued to take on additional responsibility and by 2013 I became Director of Operations. It was during this period that the leadership team read the book *Multipliers* by Liz Wiseman. That book hit me between the eyes, hard.

Wiseman observes that employees who rise within the organization on the merit of their strengths and become supervisors make a common mistake: they end up over-relying on those strengths that got them there, and in the process, end up diminishing those same strengths in their employees.

Yeah, that was me. I was, as Wiseman (and I'm sure others around me) termed it, a know-it-all. I loved to show off my smarts by being quick with answers and generous with ideas. Others would bring ideas and I would use my power of insight to shoot those concepts full of holes, killing them before they barely had a chance to breathe. Woof, right?!

Ultimately, people learned to sit back and let me do all the work. Meanwhile, I missed out on the brilliance and diverse perspectives of my team. Again and again and again.

Looking back, wincing as I do, I imagine I wasn't all that bad. Like anyone, I had plenty of good moments, ones where I was perhaps a bit more graceful than the people-pleasing-question-answering-heat-seeking-missile of a man described above.

But I'm hard on myself as I reflect on those years because I regret my blindness. Not that I'm a perfect and fully enlightened, radically emotionally intelligent guy today either, but I've made some headway for sure. And looking back with the perspective I've gained makes me wonder what things might have changed along the way if I would have been able to recognize the pull of the reins from my teacher's-pet subconscious.

The Coach

Reading *Multipliers* woke me up. Like a cold bucket of water, not pleasant, but effective. That was the first step. It was callouts and coaching that helped me make real progress moving forward.

Tony and I had a tumultuous relationship for years, up until the point where we started to understand what made us both tick and to appreciate our differences that drove each other crazy as strengths.

Tony is a big guy with a big heart. Italian-Canadian by way of Detroit. He played hockey all his life, often in the unofficial enforcer role. In the early years of our relationship, he had a quick temper. We'd argue like brothers.

Like brothers, there was real love and a sense that we were tied together and needed each other, even though we could drive each other nuts.

Tony came to work at BIGGBY in 2001. I joined Bob and Mike's team a little more than a year later in January 2003. After a year and a half, I got the opportunity to take over as the Director of Training, having deep store experience and a natural inclination to teach.

I had to build a training manual and accompanying classes for new store managers. I met Tony in one of my first classes.

I was convinced he hated me. He sat, elbows on the table, hands propping his chin, with an emotionless blank look staring me down. If I was getting through to him, I wouldn't have been able to tell you. It wasn't until years later that I came to understand that what I observed as bored disengagement was just Tony in deep concentration, trying to stay focused and absorb what was being presented. Plus, he came with years of experience, including the toughest kind, where regular customers in Toledo would inform Tony how much he and BIGGBY

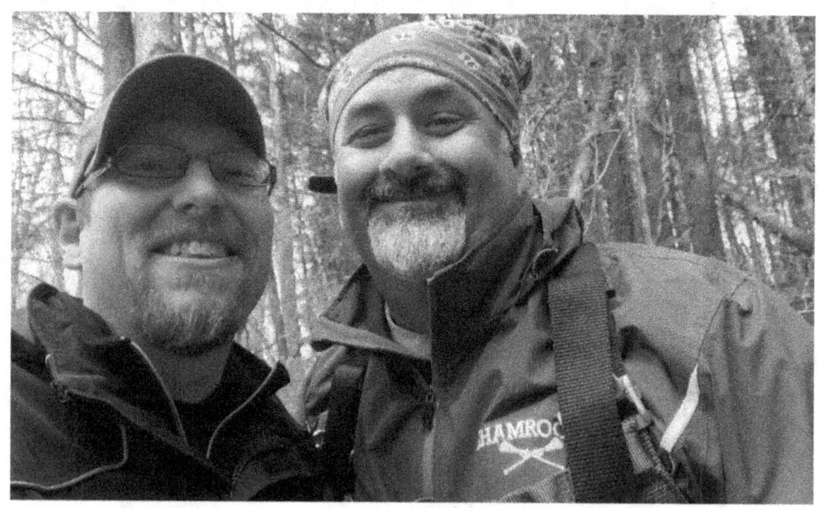

Me and Tony on a retreat with Crux Move Consulting, 2017

sucked compared to the previous (failing, I might add) brand. I'm not confident that I had much that he needed to learn.

Over time, we evolved into a dynamic duo, benefiting from each other's strengths. Tony is full of bold drive—a rule breaker, whereas I'm a rule follower. He's way better at thinking outside the box and creating solutions that can hit me like a flashbang grenade...like...I want to help you but I'm disoriented...give me a second. Then on the opposite end of the spectrum, he knew he could rely on me for thoughtful analysis, probing for challenges, and diving deep into details to help bring his ideas into three-dimensional life.

It was Tony who would call me out with equal parts annoyance and care for my bad behavior. I'd trigger him by butting in and putting words in his mouth or by answering questions aimed at others in the room. But like a good coach, he could point out the things I was doing that were hurting my performance and the team at large.

There are many more TD & JD stories, including how we turned a corner forever in our relationship. As I write this, we're seven years past that moment. We've both learned a LOT about ourselves and each other. If he brings a question or a critique about something I've done, I know it's 100 percent out of love and support and I am eager to listen. He's coaching so I can be better. If y'all don't have your own Tony, you need one. I didn't ask him for help back in the day, but I needed him. I'm grateful for the hard work he's put in to help me wake up.

Do you have your own Tony? Who loves you enough to be tough on you, when that's what you need?

Get in Motion: Your Subconscious and Waking Up

Your subconscious does all kinds of great stuff. It makes life livable by taking the pressure off your conscious mind, filtering and sorting all kinds of data and putting you on autopilot whenever possible so you can conserve energy.

It also regularly messes up your life.

This exercise is a variation on the end of the previous chapter where you identified scripts you're following. I want you to sniff around and discover your own icky and persistent behaviors that are getting in your way.

Start writing answers to these questions or grab a friend like Tony to work through your answers together.

1. Which behaviors or habits do you have that you wish you could change but have frequently failed to get traction on?
2. For each behavior or habit, think back to when you were young, say 20 and younger. Can you think of anything you might have observed as a kid that could be related?
3. By continuing the habit, how does it hurt you? How does it benefit you?
4. What have you tried in order to change? What haven't you tried?
5. What do you want to do with this information? Is there a next step you will commit to taking?`

Chapter Three

Our "Stories"

Let's talk more about our wondrous and twisty brains. In the same way our subconscious is brilliant at fitting things into patterns without any effort, the front of our brain does a lot of work without us asking for help. When we observe something and don't know what it is or what it means, our brains go to work.

Picture this like Pixar's *Inside Out*, where we got to look inside Riley's brain to see her emotions personified and standing ready at the controls in Riley's brain, but now instead of Joy and Anger and Sadness, you have Sherlock Holmes and Professor X and Nancy Drew at the helm. Our brains just love to solve mysteries and read minds.

Those three are good at their jobs and love what they do, and you don't have to ask them or compensate them to get them to go to work. They are always fast to get started solving a mystery that no one asked them to look at.

The Dreaded "K."

Here's an easy example, taken from the pre-COVID years of working in-person full time at our office.

As the workday winds down, a couple of co-workers suggest going out to grab a drink after work. I text Megan to see if she minds.

Megan replies: "K."

That's it. Just, "K." A single letter. How would you interpret that?

A. "Good to go, have fun!"

B. "That's fine, but It's going to cost you later."

C. "Roger that."

D. "I'm not happy but I won't tell you not to stay with your friends and I'm disappointed to know you're perfectly happy to scrap our plans."

E. All of the Above.

F. None of the Above.

There's no right answer. It's a single letter. She was thinking... something...when she typed "K," but I have only guesses. Nancy Drew dashes to work, rifling through memories to see if there are any clues, comparing and contrasting to previous events. Sherlock starts playing the three-dimensional chess of figuring out how to respond without making matters worse while drawing out more information. Professor X reaches across space and time with the power of his mind, searching Megan's psyche for additional clues.

Sound familiar? I'm guessing you have your own versions of this, where your brain races, looking for meaning based on scant information. We don't even have to try.

Our brains create meaning automatically and constantly.

Let's look at another example. You're in bed, getting ready to go to sleep. You hear a noise. Depending on the nature of the sound, your experience, what movie you were watching earlier that night, and many other factors, you start synthesizing stories. It was just the wind picking up or was it someone breaking in? Regardless, you react based on the story. Either your fight or flight mode might kicks in or you yawn, kill the lights, and slip away to sleep a few short moments later.

I will return to the idea that we respond to our stories instead of reality. But first, let's spend more time on our twisty and interesting brains.

The Never-Ending Novel

Our internal detectives and psychics start working overtime when we observe something that doesn't fit those patterns that our subconscious put together.

For example, I walked into my office this morning with my breakfast and coffee, turned on some chill music, and read while I ate my breakfast. I reloaded on coffee and sat in my chair, and now, ten minutes later, I'm typing these words. At no point did I take any notice of my surroundings. My eyes were open the whole time, but I paid no attention to what was going on in my office. There was no need. Everything fit—it all made sense, even though I never consciously performed a "do my surroundings make sense to me?" check.

Imagine instead, upon turning the lights, I saw one of my books in the middle of the floor? Picture me, bowl of oatmeal and coffee mug in hand, looking down at the book, then back up to the shelf, and back down again.

In the middle of my floor, the book doesn't jive with the pattern of normalcy, so my subconscious fires off a flare. My conscious brain wakes up and I focus my eyes on the book and start looking around. Sherlock, Nancy, and Xavier huddle up immediately.

After a short conference, Sherlock and Nancy narrow it to ghosts, a miniature targeted earthquake, or my wife. Professor X explains that Megan was interested in using the book for her ninth-grade students, but got distracted by a dog either being cute or throwing up and dropped the book to either cuddle the dog or get her off the carpet and onto the hardwood.

With a plausible explanation, I would then be able to replace the book, take a mental note to ask Megan later, and then go about my business.

Get this though: up until "later" with Megan, I'm actually living in a reality that I created.

Our stories become our reality.

I observed a book on the ground and invented a story to explain it. That story would be a small entry in the never-ending novel that my brain writes, sometimes in my awareness, most often deep in the background of the machinery of my mind.

Our brains are beautiful, fascinating, and just-a-little-bit-terrifying because of the power that's thrumming under the hood.

Weighed Down By Our Past

Our brains can construct our reality by building patterns and writing stories to explain the stuff that doesn't fit. But we're not nearly done with our twisty little grey matter's ability to influence our daily lives.

While our brains make meaning of what's going on, they also have the pesky habit of pulling us out of the present moment, forgetting our surroundings entirely!

How often do you think about the future or the past? How much anxiety do you carry? How much guilt or resentment do you feel? Guess what? Anxiety comes from being stuck in the future. Guilt and resentment are you rooted in your storied-up versions of the past. Once more: how often do you think about the past or the future?

The answer: "Multiple times a day, maybe more than I can count, every day."

Not your fault, friend. It's just that twisty troublemaker doing what it does best...thinking. Some of us are more prone to ruminating and anxiety than others, but we are all vulnerable.

Many of us are inflicting damage to ourselves today for what happened weeks, months, or even years ago.

We are the victim and perpetrator. We suffered from the actions of another. It was unfair. Painful. Embarrassing. Wrong. A violation. It happened. You bore the consequences. You didn't deserve what happened, and the pain you carried forward through your life is justified.

But I need you to hear this: What happened...happened. Past tense. What you feel today...pain, guilt, embarrassment, anger, shame—all valid reactions—are all self-imposed. All self-perpetuated. All the product of your brain doing what it does best...thinking and feeling.

We were hurt and we continue to hurt ourselves because of it. We are both victim and perpetrator.

If you can come to terms with the idea that what happened... happened, and you leave the past where it belongs, you will gain a new sense of freedom. Easily said, right? It will take work and depending on what you're carrying, could require professional help. Get started on this work. The burden of trauma prevents us from living our fullest life.

When people come to grips with this idea that the past is actually behind them, they visibly transform. Like watching a person relieved of 150 pounds, one heavy wet blanket at a time. They straightened their backs. They squared their shoulders. They looked up and looked around, seeing and being seen. They reclaimed themselves... from themselves. The weight no longer controls them. They are not victims. It's the same with the past. The past no longer controls you.

For me, this is another example of writing stories. In the same way I wrote a story about a one-letter "K" text message or a misplaced book on the floor, we also write stories about our past. Our subconscious keeps going! It assembles another story, a sequel, if you will. The first entry is: "This thing happened in our past." The sequel reads, "And so, the entire world has changed as a result, react accordingly."

The truth is: The rest of the world continues as it was, but because you're now living inside this story you've written, you change how you walk through the world. The type of story you write will inform how you behave. Will you write something that's crippling? Empowering? You have a choice whether you can see it or not!

The Locker Room Trap

You'll recall I was a teacher's pet. Lots of classes with the word "advanced" or "honors" in their names.

I was in the eighth grade when I took algebra alongside a couple dozen classmates. Despite having no memory of the classwork, I must have done well because in ninth grade, I found myself in geometry. With one other freshman. Where did my classmates from algebra go? No idea. It was just me and one other freshman and loads of sophomores, juniors, and seniors.

I don't have memories of the math work from this class either. I sat toward the rear left-hand side of the room. I remember the teacher was weak, nearing retirement and frequently overrun and outmatched by the loud upperclassmen. What my teacher-wife would call "zero classroom management."

I assume I did my usual quick-with-the-answer-teacher's-pet routine. It's also a good bet the upperclassmen, a year or two behind in math, weren't jazzed to be in that windowless math dungeon. They were much more at home in the weight room, as I would discover the following year when I took "Team Sports" aka gym class.

I enjoyed gym class, aside from the suicide sprints. It didn't matter which sport we were playing—chances were good I'd enjoy myself. Floor hockey, basketball, soccer, baseball, kickball, dodgeball, golf, and tennis were all enjoyable because I got to practice hitting the mark. I thrive on challenge.

The difficulty was that I had gym class the same hour that some of those geometry upperclassmen had weightlifting. Which put us in the locker room together.

I was uneasy in the locker room anyway. What teenager doesn't when herded together into a locker room? I suppose that ultra-confident specimen exists, but it's hard to imagine, given how I felt.

The locker room is where I remember being bullied the worst. It happened everywhere, especially those first two years, but the locker room was different.

Here were those same upperclassmen who I imagine were completely annoyed with me from Geometry. They'd spent the hour lifting weights, listening to 90's era metal, their mullets slick with sweat, practically drowning in their own testosterone.

I was an easy target. Bespectacled teacher's pet, smaller than them, and in the locker room I was far from the protective aura of any teachers. I was trapped.

There are plenty of kids who have been bullied so much worse than I was. I grew up a white cis gender heterosexual boy in the era before social media. I factually know I didn't have it so bad. Tell that to 15-year-old me and I'm not sure that I would have been able to imagine.

Experiences like that—like when we are bullied—are the breeding ground for the stories we write about ourselves and the world at large.

Nearly 30 years later, I'm poking around in my brain for the stories I wrote because of the bullying. Okay, let's try an experiment. I'll think of the stories a kid like me could have formed, given that locker room setup:

- I'm weak.
- I don't fit in.
- There's something wrong with me.
- I deserve the abuse.
- No one will stick up for me or rescue me. I'm alone.

Looking at the list, I didn't write any of those stories for myself. Why didn't I internalize any of those self-defeating, self-limiting beliefs? It's because my mom armed me with an empowering story that I'd already taken in as truth: "People who bully you are just jealous of you."

We form beliefs that hold us back from our fullest potential. But guess what?

We have an equal ability to tell ourselves stories that give us freedom and give us power.

My mom told me that bullies are just jealous, so I walked away from all those bad experiences with the idea that it's not because there's something wrong with me, it's because there's something right about me.

It's all just a story! It prevented me from absorbing any of those five hurtful stories above. Any one of them could have become a self-limiting belief that could have weighed me down for the last 30 years of my life.

What stories are you carrying around? Are they giving you power and freedom or weighing you down? This activity will help you discover your stories and then you can start rewriting them for yourself.

Get in Motion: Rewriting Your Stories

Jen Sincero had great advice in *You Are a Badass*, pointing out that in a where-there's-smoke-there's-fire way, if you find yourself thinking thoughts that begin with phrases like "I always..." "I never..." "I should..." "I shouldn't..." or "I can't..." you might be smelling a self-limiting belief smoldering in your subconscious.

So, let's look at different areas of life and activities and see if anything comes up for you when you consider each prompt. Write down anything you find.

1. In my family, I always...I never...I should...I shouldn't...I can't...
2. With my friends, I always...I never...I should...I shouldn't...I can't...
3. At work, I always...I never...I should...I shouldn't...I can't...
4. Physically, I always...I never...I should...I shouldn't...I can't...
5. Mentally, I always...I never...I should...I shouldn't...I can't...
6. Emotionally, I always...I never...I should...I shouldn't...I can't...
7. Spiritually, I always...I never...I should...I shouldn't...I can't...
8. Around the house, I always...I never...I should...I shouldn't...I can't...
9. When it comes to money, I always...I never...I should...I shouldn't...I can't...
10. In my love life, I always...I never...I should...I shouldn't...I can't...

Okay, how are we feeling? The first time I did this activity, it made me sad to see all of those constraints I'd been carrying around in my life, each one like a ghostly wet blanket, dimming my sight and weighing me down.

If that's where you are, give yourself a hug and then let's

get to work. We're going to wring the unreality out of your wet blankets. For each statement you wrote, it's time to do a reality check. What's the truth? And what more is possible?

For example:

- I shouldn't share my real opinions with my family -> I worry that my family won't accept me as I really am, but I know that if I do, they love me and I trust that love will keep us together.
- Physically, I can't run a marathon -> I can't run a marathon today, but if I commit myself to training and am patient with my progress, I could totally complete a marathon.
- When it comes to money, I'll never earn enough to have the things I want -> I'm stuck in my thinking about my career path and need to broaden my horizon for different ways I could put my skills, experience, and passion to work; I should consult with a recruiter.

Chapter Four

What a Worldview

Now that you've uncovered some stories you've been carrying around and how they affect your worldview, it's time to take that work to its next logical step: to realize that each and every other person around you has their own stories. When you do, it's easy to extend grace to others. Oh, and a side benefit: it will help you to stay sane and keep your cool when you need it the most.

We're All the Hero of Our Own Story

Does the name "Elphaba" ring a bell for you? If not, perhaps you know her by her alter ego: The Wicked Witch of the West?

Gregory Maguire published *Wicked: The Life and Times of the Wicked Witch of the West* in 1995, which went on to become a hit Broadway musical in 2003, has since climbed into fifth place for longest running musical ever, and soon will be released as a pair of movies.

I enjoyed the book and its Broadway adaptation. It tells the story of a talented and misunderstood outsider, Elphaba, and her journey through university to eventually becoming the feared Wicked Witch. This retelling of the Wizard of Oz story reorients our perspective on the one-dimensional cackling villain from the 1939 film (or perhaps you read the Oz books?) and turns her into a completely sympathetic character. A victim, even.

It's a fun device to take a well-known story and setting and re-imagine it from another angle. Megan and I just got done watching *The Book of Boba Fett* series. A multi-million dollar 7-episode series built around a character who scores a total of four lines in the original *Star Wars* trilogy. *Better Call Saul*, a spinoff series from *Breaking Bad*, centering around a minor character, schlocky attorney Saul Goodman, is entering its sixth season at the time of writing, exceeding *Breaking Bad*, which finished its own successful and suspenseful run at just five seasons.

Those are just a few Hollywood-style examples of a principle you should repeat like a mantra:

Everyone is the hero of their own story.

It's easy to become trapped inside our own perspective and forget that everyone we encounter is a fully developed person with their own history, stories, challenges, and dreams. It's obvious when stated that plainly...like, yeah, of course they are. But do you go through your day conscious of that?

If you have a crummy customer experience at the grocery store, how much time do you spend wondering about that cashier and their story? Or are you focused on the extra eight seconds they burned while talking to the cashier in the next lane and the hurry you're in and why does everything have to be so hard and why can't the kids just get themselves ready for school anyway and why am I the one who has to take the dogs out in the morning, etc. etc. etc.?

We get trapped in our own story while forgetting everyone else has one too.

Remember the other person in the equation—even though in the movie of your life they're merely an extra with a single line of dialogue—they are at the center of their very own story. If we can keep that front of mind, it can help us find a little bit of grace for people when they need it.

"A-Hole" to "Hospital"

When you have an encounter with someone who irritates or angers you, take a moment. Try to imagine they have something going on in their life that would make their behavior understandable. This is another example of how we can write a more empowering/freeing story.

My first encounter with this thinking came from a story from Stephen R. Covey in the first chapter of *The 7 Habits of Highly Effective People*. He had an epiphany while riding a New York City subway. Two kids were running amok, annoying Covey and disturbing other passengers while their father stared blankly, ignoring the kids' antics. Covey was wrapped in his thoughts and writing stories about what an unthinking, inconsiderate, failure-of-a-parent this dad was until he decided to address the issue directly. He confronts the dad, asking him to get his kids under control, only to find out they were on the way home from the hospital where his wife, the mother of the unruly kids, had died.

Can you guess what happened? It's easy to imagine ourselves in his shoes - we've all been annoyed and wanted to chide someone for bad behavior. With one piece of information, Covey's perspective shifted completely. His annoyance drained away, replacing the desire to chide with a need to help.

What if Covey had begun with that assumption? I know, I know, I know. That would make him a weird and macabre dude, assuming tragedy at the drop of a hat. But still, as a thought experiment, in those first minutes if Covey made a different assumption he would have written a different story. If he intentionally chose a different perspective to believe, he would have felt and behaved differently.

That passage in Covey's book led me to my own experiment. Megan and I bought property and built a house outside of Grand Rapids, MI, just a bit out in the country. I loved it because we had four acres for me to play on and it put us closer to our friends and family. The only downside was my commute going from 50 minutes round-trip to two hours.

That means for seven years, up until the COVID-19 pandemic shifted most of the BIGGBY Home Office to remote work, I was on the road for ten hours a week. Thankfully, this isn't the kind of nonsense my friends who live in the Detroit area or in other big cities have to deal with. At least my two hours on the road were spent, you know, driving, and not in bumper-to-bumper traffic.

That time on the road offered a lot of opportunity for me. Plenty of time to get my head on straight before stepping into the office, and an equal amount of time to shift gears before walking in the door to spend the evening with Megan. Time for phone calls, particularly calls to Mom, which became part of the weekly routine. Audiobooks quickly became 90 percent of my book diet. There was also plenty of time available to see the worst that Michigan drivers had to offer.

While it's true that slow drivers in the passing lane rank amongst my biggest pet peeves, the experiences that set the stage for my Covey-inspired experiment involved drivers who frightened me. Particularly the drivers who would make a sudden lane change, cutting me off, to speed ahead and pass one of those aforementioned left-lane cruisers in the right lane. They startled me, they upset me, and they made me angry.

My heart would race from the startle and having to slam on my brakes. I'd curse out the other driver. My knuckles would go white as I clenched the steering wheel. Jaw completely locked. I'd speed up, not quite tailgating, but definitely not letting them get away. I thought by sticking with him, he'd know what he did. I'd back off after a little bit, but I'd still be upset, just strangling my steering wheel. Minutes would pass, the audiobook narrator reading, but I wasn't listening.

After I read that first chapter in *7 Habits*, and after the billionth time I'd been cut off, I realized that I had an opportunity. I could tell myself a different story. I told myself that he was trying to get to the hospital. That was it. I didn't need any more context. It wasn't about a baby being born, or a family member badly injured, just the one word in my mind: "hospital."

With this perspective, here's what would happen: My heart would race from the startle and having to slam on my brakes. I'd curse out the other driver. My knuckles would go white as I clenched the steering wheel. Jaw completely locked. I'd speed up, not quite tailgating, and then I'd remember "hospital." And my foot would ease off the gas, and I'd release my death grip on the wheel, and I'd begin to be able to hear the audiobook again, and my heart rate would slow. I could feel my body release the tension. Because of a story I told to myself.

Over time, I became well-practiced at this. My initial response always stayed the same – I would startle and slam on the brakes. With all those repetitions, however, the lag time between that stimulus and my new reflex shortened. Which meant the amount of time I spent in stress, being angry, not hearing my audiobook, shortened. It got to the point where it was one right after the other, like dominos falling. I reclaimed hours of my life by making that adjustment. More importantly, it taught me the power of my own mind. I can tweak my perspective a little bit and give myself emotional freedom.

An Honest Perspective

I imagine that in 2020 in the United States, perhaps across the world, every single person experienced the same phenomenon: staring at the screen, slack-jawed, confused, and maybe a little angry. COVID had already pushed many of us into a kind of isolation we couldn't have understood just a few months before. The presidential election pulled us into separate camps. The murder of George Floyd brought social justice and systemic racism to the front of our public conversation. It was incredibly easy to find yourself on the opposite side of an argument with someone you love.

That's not dramatic enough. I bet records were set in 2020 for unfriending and unfollowing on social media. It was a polarizing year. Many retreated into their own ideological bubble.

I'm a level-headed guy. Not prone to big swings of emotion. Yet there were a bunch of times that year when I was pissed. I found myself repeating two phrases a lot, both to myself and to the people around me, to help me keep perspective and to avoid going off the deep end.

The first phrase came from Brenè Brown's *Braving the Wilderness*:

"People are hard to hate up close."

She makes the point that when you sit down and talk with another person who has different views, you are confronted with the full complexity of them as a human being with all of their good points and endearing qualities, making it much more difficult to write them off as ignorant, confused, or evil. People are hard to hate up close.

She's right. I consider myself fortunate that most of my family is on the opposite end of the political spectrum from me. It helps to ground me in a way that when I hear someone in my life or on social media going off on conservatives, I can push back when it feels like the other person has lost perspective of the lived and tender humanity on the "other side of the aisle." I love my family. I see them for who they are, not just how they vote. I'm up close.

The other phrase that I found myself repeating is one that I coined once while in a coaching session: "Everyone comes about their perspective honestly." This is a close relative to "everyone is the hero of their own story." Every moment of your life, while your subconscious worked away, fitting pieces into the ever-growing puzzle and as your conscious brain wrote stories and solved mysteries, you were glacially forming your present-day perspective. Whether you knew it or not, you've been learning lessons from every conversation, every dream, every disappointment, all the movies you've watched, plus the tv shows, books, and social media posts...all of it.

The sum total of all of those conscious decisions and subconscious scribblings is your worldview. The lens through which you experience everything.

Everyone comes about their perspective honestly.

The difficulty is that we have a natural bias to believe that the way that we see the world is capital-R Right and that others are either confused or capital-W-R-O-N-G Wrong. That's the part that gets us into trouble.

It's completely natural, though. I cannot emphasize this enough. Here's a low-stakes version of this. Many of my friends and coworkers at BIGGBY grew up in the Detroit area. I grew up on the other side of the state near Grand Rapids. The house we lived in was a two-story with a walkout basement. We had a glass door leading out to a deck and another like it that led out to the basement/backyard patio. The glass doors are large and are on a track, and they slide back and forth on the track to open and close, as opposed to all the other hinged doors in our house. We called those big glass doors "sliding doors." Because, you know, they slide. The lovely humans whom I'm friends with and work with from the Detroit area insist that it isn't a sliding door, it's a "doorwall."

Doorwall? No. No, no, no. I am Right and they are Wrong. Like, I get the equivalent logic of doorwall. Just like it being a door that slides, it is also sufficiently large enough to be wall-like. But that's a silly made-up name for it and my version is correct.

It's just so easy to start from a position of: "No, that's not right, you are wrong" when confronted with something that completely contradicts all of the lessons of your own life. Here's another small and trivial example, also based on words: A little while into our marriage, after buying our first home, we paid to have a contractor come and finish our basement. It would become the hangout space of the house, a place to watch movies, play video games, and play board games. When the job was done, we needed a table to play games on down there, so we went out and bought a black set of folding chairs and a folding table. Do you know another name for that kind of table?

So at some point, my ear caught a distinction when Megan would talk about the table, something like "Oh, hey, honey, we should bring the cart table with us this weekend." Huh? What was that? Did she say what I think she did? "Say again?" "We should bring the carT table this weekend."

Now, I don't know about you, but I grew up referring to that kind of table and chairs as a card table. So when I drilled in with Megan, with the corner of my mouth fighting back a smirk, we quickly established that she was prepared to die on Cart Table Hill. I retreated to Google and she brought in reinforcements, calling her sister, who confirmed, yes, that's absolutely a cart table. Google and its millions of hits were on my side. Cart tables do exist, with wheels on two of their legs, but, you know, that's literally a whole different thing.

Again, this is a trivial matter where the—ahem—table stakes are whoever "wins" gets to leave the conversation with smirk intact. We went into the conversation equally convinced that our position was the correct one, and the other person was Wrong, based on all the data points we'd gathered in our lives before that moment.

That was a case where there actually is a verifiable right and wrong answer, where Google was able to quickly settle things and neither of us were going to lose any sleep over the outcome. People bring that same level of certainty to debates where the answers are much murkier and the stakes much higher.

The next time you find yourself staring slack-jawed at your screen or clenching your fists in the middle of a heated debate, try to remind yourself that the other person has come about that perspective honestly, just like you.

Get in Motion: Working with Perspective

We have a tendency, as humans, to get stuck inside our own perspective. Let's see if we can't shake that up with a few activities.

Ready, Aim, Complain!

I hope you're feeling a little grouchy right now. It might help with this first part. Get ready to write a little bit. Go ahead and list out all of your complaints in life. No, really. Gripe like you've never griped before.

Seeing the Other Side

Once you've completed your list of complaints, it's time to go to work on seeing the other side of the problems you've written down. Look at each one.

- If it's a complaint about another person, I want you to start imagining a story that would make the person's actions reasonable, maybe even excusable. Just like Covey and the widower on the subway—what might explain the other person's actions? Remember, they're the hero of their own story!
- If it's a complaint about you, I want you to look at that problem from the perspective of someone else who would feel grateful to have that problem. For example, if you have a broken toe that's got you down, imagine how grateful an amputee would feel to have that problem instead.

Making It A Reflex

Now look over your list of complaints and try to find one or two that you bump up against frequently in your daily life, like me with getting cut off on the freeway. Think through the story you imagined before and come up with a word that sums it up, like "Hospital" did for me. That's the word I want you to use to build your new reflex.

At first, you might not remember until later in your day, but I still want you to say that word to yourself. Because this is a frequent irritant, you'll get practice at it, and the lag time between the stimulus and your new intentional reflex will shorten. Enjoy the freedom you create for yourself!

Note: If the problem that you have with another person is someone in your life and not some public figure or anonymous driver on the freeway, and your complaint is rooted in an assumption you've made about them (like assuming they have ill intent), you have extra work to do.

While writing a new story and turning it into a reflex will give you relief, the better thing to do is to go to that person (which takes courage) and talk to them about what you've observed. Own up to the assumption that you've been holding against them. Ask them to tell the story from their perspective, and just see what you might learn!

It takes more work, but checking your assumption gives you the opportunity to disappear that complaint for good!

Chapter Five

The Nasty Bits Beneath the Surface

Nice work there. You're starting to get the hang of how you can reframe the world around you to give yourself freedom. Before you take a victory lap, it's time to consider the uglier things you've got going on just beneath the surface of that worldview you've built.

Now that you know you're seeing the world through your honestly-gained perspective—and so too is everyone else—I'm guessing you have noticed the struggle bus pulling up when you're interacting with someone who is coming at things from a totally different perspective.

What's that all about? If we can understand intellectually that everyone has their own lens, why don't we walk through life with an endless amount of grace on hand to give to people when they do something bonkers? It's that under-the-hood-of-us-all ugliness that's to blame. Let's look at some of the unhelpful behaviors we've all built along the way.

Alright, Judgy McJudgerton

There's a further aspect to the whole "I'm Right and you're Wrong" thing. The things that you view as W-R-O-N-G Wrong—the things you notice about others that burrow under your skin and irritate you—are a problem for you because they're likely a problem with you. Just look a little closer, not just at them, but at yourself, to see if it's something about yourself that you're uncomfortable or unhappy with.

I can't help but think of *Top Chef* as I write. Megan and I are huge fans of the show. We've rewatched all of the seasons multiple times. There's a contestant from season one who drives me bonkers. Stephen. The sommelier. In one of the first challenges, he insists on finding the perfect wine pairing to go with his dish, and he does that mysterious thing that wine aficionados do with the aggressive swirling and the nose buried deep in the glass thing as he searches for the wine-soulmate for his entree.

The interviews and editing of the show set him up as the antagonist, so I recognize that my issue with Stephen isn't solely a me-thing. But every episode we watch, I'm guaranteed to groan, roll my eyes, and comment on how awful he is. He's clearly knowledgeable, one of the better-prepared contestants in his season, but, just, wow. He cannot help but flaunt that knowledge. Flaunt, even, is too tame a word for what Stephen does. He assaults people with his knowledge. This isn't me saying "he's so knowledgeable, he's a ninja, a master, he slays, etc." This is me saying that he is the culinary equivalent of a flasher. It's an affront to decency. Completely unwanted.

So why does this get under my skin? I hate admitting this, but I feel like Stephen is the nightmare version of the part of me that takes pride in what I know and wants to share it. Sharing what I've learned is virtuous and it's other-focused and it is me at my best. The desire to show off what I know is needy and me-focused and a sign of me feeling insecure. That's what I see in Stephen. That's why

I hate-watch my way through every scene he's in. He drives me crazy because he reminds me of what I could be if my worst self achieves its final Pokémon form.

If you find yourself getting uptight about how someone else is behaving, it's worth a look in the mirror.

Is it a reflection of a part of yourself that you don't like?

Another possibility: The judgment you made about the other person—especially if that person is someone close to you—is an expression of need buried under one-hundred pounds of ego-protecting armor...

A Tragic Expression

The team I'm on at BIGGBY is called the Life You Love Laboratory, or LifeLab for short. We develop tools and share practices that help people to build lives they love—we are full-time living out the BIGGBY purpose. We lead workshops for BIGGBY employees and the public at large. In one of them, we delve into the subject of vulnerability. One of the videos we discuss is a TEDxAmsterdam presentation from Yoram Mosenzon titled "Vulnerable Honesty."

The first time that I watched it, I got hit between the eyes by a quote that Yoram shares from Marshall Rosenberg: "Every judgment is a tragic expression of an unmet need." He gives examples where he is reacting to his girlfriend in a snappish way, which I'm sorry to say, I relate to.

It's the area of growth I'm most focused on. I have recognized that I have a nasty habit and poor Megan bears the brunt of it. If I perceive some kind of threat from a person, I want to return fire immediately. It's often something small, but in the moment I feel like I'm taking a jab, so I hit right back.

Come with me on a journey into my pettiness.

I have gotten upset with my wife for being passive and for being "passive-aggressive." That phrase gets quotes because she's not being passive-aggressive. That's how I receive it. I don't like typing any of those words, but it's true. I get upset and I hold her in judgment because of it. We have talked about this over the years. There are little phrases that would trigger me because I felt they were so indirect and that she wasn't saying what she meant.

"Honey, do you want to take out the dogs?" Do I want to? No, I would not. I would like to stay in this comfy chair and keep playing my video game. So, I'd get this little flash of anger about her phrasing and I would dig in on her for being indirect. I'd go back at her: "Do I want to? Don't you really mean, 'Would you please take the dogs out? I did it last time?' " So petty, Jeremy! Yeesh!

Now you might look at the directness/indirectness of the language and you might want to "side" with me on that. Okay, you can do that, but let's pause to examine the real issue at hand: Why was I getting angry? There's no reason to be upset about those combinations of words. So that should tell you it's not about the words, it's not about Megan, it's about me.

Every judgment is a tragic expression of an unmet need.

Looking back at those moments, I can see a lot that I wasn't conscious of at the time.

You will recall my struggles with interpreting the Dreaded K from chapter three. That's part of a larger pattern for me that is tied to a need. Because I'm so good at imagining alternate possibilities (which is a genuine strength when used for the powers of good), it means I have a strong preference for clear and direct communication. I want to make sure that the way I'm hearing you is correct—in other words: I want to make sure I've constructed your intended meaning.

My time as a coach has given me a lot of practice at listening for vague language and asking follow-up questions for clarity. "Who is 'we'?" "What do you mean by 'good?'" "When you say that you're 'not getting support,' what does 'support' mean to you?"

Not only do I have a built-in need for clear language to keep me from spinning out on the possible meanings, I also have developed a reflex to want to dissect meaning in real-time. End result: Megan asks what in her mind is a nonthreatening, purely functional let's-get-from-Point-A-to-Point-B-in-our-day question, and I short circuit because I don't hear the question as intended and respond with my ridiculous anger.

These little exchanges of fire (I picture a Continental Army of tiny Jeremys firing their muskets at neatly ordered ranks of micro Megans and then vice versa) can erode a marriage if you're not careful. Thankfully, Megan and I are careful and caring people, so it doesn't escalate. I realize as soon as the words have flown that I was being mean. I'll apologize, or if I'm still upset it will take me a while. But we do a good job of abiding by the "don't go to bed angry" rule.

When we're at our best, Megan and I warn each other that we're crabby before the mini muskets come out.

As I said before, this is an area of my emotional life that I'm actively working on. "Actively" means that this concept lives close to the front of my brain, so when opportunities arise (read: when I get sassy and/or judgmental with someone) I'm often conscious of what I have going on inside. "Working on it" means that from one opportunity to the next, I am getting faster at recognizing my emotions.

Here's what that looks like:

5 years ago: I get all sassy and uptight about it and need time away from Megan before I can reset. I may or may not have apologized, depending on the specifics of the exchange.

1 year ago: I get all sassy and uptight about it and on rare occasions need time away to reset. I am much more conscious of being short with her, and almost guaranteed to apologize.

3 months ago: I get all sassy and uptight but realize what I'm doing right after I get short with her, apologize immediately, and am able to articulate what just happened to help us both understand my built-in reaction.

Right now: I get all sassy and uptight about it and sometimes catch myself before I even say the thing. Because I'm able to catch myself before damage is done in those good moments, Megan's army never even realizes that mine was mustering for battle. So, she doesn't get upset, doesn't fire back, and I don't need to go on the defensive or apologize. As a result, I spend much less time feeling upset. It's similar to the dynamic I described about "A-hole" to "Hospital." My response time is speeding up and I'm getting better results for myself (and Megan) as a result.

Dear reader, I don't have everything figured out. Heck, I even have a goblin or two burrowed away in my brain, as you'll read about in the next chapter. I'm absolutely a work in progress, and proud of it.

And how about you? Reflect on where you've been in your emotional self-awareness journey.

Where have you seen progress? Something that may have once gotten under your skin, but you've found ways to avoid a spiral? Or perhaps you've found a way to be able explain how you're feeling and that act of naming it helps you gain some self-control or solicit extra support from the people around you? Where have you seen wins and what do you want to start actively working on?

Your Ugly Little Goblin

Brace yourself. I've got more behind-the-curtains-of-your-brain ugliness to draw to your attention. Sorry about that. Ah, being human.

Because you're human, I bet you have some areas in life where you are dissatisfied. Where you have bad habits you cannot shake. Destructive patterns that play on repeat in your life. Are you nodding a solid—maybe even shameful-— "Yes" to that assertion?

Okay, cool, welcome to the club. It's not exclusive. We have billions of members from every nation and walk of life. You are welcome here.

You've probably had conversations with yourself that start with "Ugh, I really shouldn't, but..." What's that about? Maybe you know that impulse is coming from a place inside you that needs some work? But I bet you keep doing it, again and again and again, despite the "I really shouldn't" moment.

The nasty part is that deep down, well below the surface, that behavior is providing you with some sort of unconscious reward. It's like you have an ugly little goblin burrowed in your brain. Even though you, in the front "thinking part" of your brain, don't want to keep on doing that thing, the goblin is totally addicted to it. He pulls that lever inside your brain every time to get that same reward. If and when you unearth him from your psyche, you're going to hate looking at that nasty little booger.

It's not your fault. Your brain is trying to keep you together and moving forward. Somewhere along the way, it invited the goblin in because it thought he was there to do good work. So, he dug in deep and has been pulling that same troublesome lever in your brain's machinery ever since.

Start by thinking about the behaviors and habits you have that you know you should change. You've maybe even made several halfway decent attempts at change. But you keep coming back, doing the thing again and again. You say "I'm gonna' change" And then you don't. Wash, rinse, and repeat. For years.

Sound familiar?

Why does the bad habit persist if you want to change it? I'll tell you: it's that deep-down-way-under-the-surface reward. It keeps the goblin going. If you find the goblin and its reward you have a chance to make the change permanent. Dragging it up into the light will help you get rid of it for good.

To find your goblin, identify the hidden reward you're getting from your persistent bad habit.

So here we go. Let's go looking for one of my goblins in the hope that it will help you to be able to identify one or more of your own.

For me, it's beer. I love it, I do. I started drinking beer in college. The kind that wins the award for the "how much can we get for as little money as possible" challenge. Beer that includes "Ice" in its title. Later, my roommate and I started messing around with imported beer like Killians, Newcastle, and Xingu before finding Kalamazoo-based Bell's Amber—my entry point into craft breweries.

I've never looked back. Sure, I enjoy a Pabst alongside pizza or wings, or the Bud Lite someone hands me at a barbecue or baseball game, but 98 percent of my consumption is the fancy (and extra fattening) brews. Above all, I love me some IPAs and use them to judge a brewery's worth.

The problem with me and beer is three-fold. It's 1) so tasty that I never want just one, 2) it's calorific, and 3) it's carb-y as all get-out. The calculus on those three things adds up to why I'm carrying this beer belly of mine.

I know it's a problem, and yet it persists.

Let's go goblin hunting. What is the deep-down hidden reward he provides?

The Nasty Bits Beneath the Surface

Oh man, this is hard, and I think I'm going to have to bring in my coach, Brie, or a therapist to help me root around in my brain to find the little creep. Here's what I've found on my own:

- I enjoy the taste of beer. But I also enjoy the taste of many other beverages, be it coffee, tea, La Croix, wine, Scotch, bourbon, and so on, but none of them pose the same issue for me. So that's not it.
- I enjoy the variety. I keep a well-stocked beer fridge with multiple styles and brands, but I know that I enjoy it. That's not a hidden reward, and it's not ugly enough to be the stuff of goblins.
- Drinking good beer allows me to signal that I care about quality. Okay, that's pretentious and I didn't like writing it, so that's ugly and goblin-y. But I've known that for a long time and have been teased by friends plenty about it. It's not hidden, so I must keep searching.
- Everything is better with beer. Okay, that's just simply not true. I do not want beer with my breakfast. But I'm always happy to have beer with lunch, a snack, dinner, or dessert. It's for celebration and consolation. It's great for hanging out with friends or family. It's nice to have when working outdoors on a summer day for a project. Getting the picture? I can always find an excuse for beer. I didn't like writing any of that either, so I might be getting warmer, but I don't really see the hidden reward here, so I think the goblin might be nearby, but this isn't it.
- I like the feeling of a good beer buzz. That would make sense wouldn't it? But I know that's not it because I rarely drink enough to get a buzz. Plus, if it's about feeling buzzy there are other less-caloric ways to achieve that kind of feeling and none of those options tempt me.

- It's a part of my identity and I like being known as a beer snob. Okay, that's gross to admit. The reward could be the feeling of pride I get when someone acknowledges that. But that might explain it if this was a behavior that was only an issue when I was in social situations. It isn't.
- It's a surefire way to stay fat, which is a comfortable part of my identity. Okay, that one hurt. So, let's play around with it. Drinking reaffirms my not trying on my fitness. Beer is the problem, right? So why worry about the boneless wings and fries? Beer pulls focus from all the other shenanigans, but because it's cloaked in a few identify-affirming things, it gives all the other crud I'm eating a free pass.

That's as far as I was able to get on my own goblin hunt. You'll see I found some things that I think are proper ugly, but known, so they don't fit the bill. Ditto the things that are ugly, but don't seem to come with a reward, so aren't likely the actual goblin. Maybe just his droppings. Turds? Yeah, pretty sure a goblin would leave a turd, not droppings.

As I said, my next step is to have my friend and coach dig in on this with me, because I'm not confident I can find that little booger on my own.

Get in Motion: Find Your Goblin(s)

It's only fair: It's your turn. And you'll be better for it, even though the process is unpleasant. It's time to do a little goblin hunting.

You guessed it, it's time to do some more writing. Ready?

1. What are the areas of life where you're dissatisfied? Where do you find yourself saying "I wish..." or "I really should..."?
2. If your list is short, you either deserve a high five and a hug for being exceptional at life or you need to be more fearless

or thorough in your introspection.

3. Once you have your list, which have been hanging on the longest in your life? Or which have you tried to change, and failed, the most?
4. Looking at what you identified in #3, which would be easiest to change? Which would be the most difficult?
5. Pick the easiest or the most difficult, whichever you want to go to work on first.
6. Here comes the hard part. You know you don't like that you do this thing. But you keep on doing it. Take an inventory of all the possible rewards your goblin is addicted to. Take a hard look at yourself. What do you think you and the goblin are getting out of the bargain? What's the payoff that keeps him pulling that lever?
7. Look at what you wrote. If you see something upsetting, you probably got it right. If nothing hits that mark, you need to keep digging, and you might need a friend who can ask you the tough questions.

When you do find that thing that the goblin is addicted to that makes you a little sick to look at, your work is done. Pulling it up to the surface is the hard part. Now that you've seen it, your goblin will be putting in for time off from working that lever. Congratulations!

VISION

Chapter Six

Energy

I have never been more tired than I was a month ago. I got a text from Mom on a Friday morning, saying that she barely had the strength to lift the blender pitcher off the base to pour her smoothie.

She had been diagnosed with ALS about three months before that moment. At the point of diagnosis, she'd already been dealing with a right arm and hand that had become powerless (an extra bummer, as she was right-handed) and speech that had become slurred. She had been bravely taking care of herself with help from her sister on household chores once or twice a week, along with my brother and I visiting every few weeks to help with chores that were heavier lifts.

But now she couldn't lift her (what...five pounds maybe?) full blender. She was scared. I would be too. That was her major meal of the day, packed with calories, fat, and protein, and to suddenly be worried about making it would mean she would struggle to get the calories she needed to try to fight back the illness. She was already having a difficult time swallowing water and some types of food. The thick drinkable smoothie was the centerpiece of her diet.

I met Jonathan (my brother) and his girlfriend at Mom's house, and we all started talking about what to do. We researched in-home care and how to bring in someone to help out with breakfast and dinner as well as other odd jobs. We left with the plan that I'd be back tomorrow and Sunday, morning and night, to test out the in-home care idea.

Saturday worked out okay, all things considered. Not that it was especially easy—it was a change in plans laced with fear for the future—but as a test of paying someone to come over and help, it worked out just fine. Until I got the call from Mom Sunday morning that she lacked the strength to get out of bed.

What followed went by in a blur. I got to the house and helped get her out of bed. Everything had changed. I didn't leave the house for the next five days.

Jonathan and Melissa came up from Chicago and gave me a 34-hour respite. I went home. Slept. Woke up next to my wife, enjoyed a nice breakfast that we made together, and cuddled with the pups. Worked out. Played my video game for a bit. Ended the day with Megan for dinner out and a concert—our first since the pandemic began two years earlier.

I returned to Mom grateful to have spent 34 hours doing things that refilled my bucket. I went into the new week with my head sitting straighter on my shoulders. It was still difficult and scary and heart-breaking to be there in that way for Mom, but it forced me to get really intentional about spending the scant amount of time I had to myself each day doing things that made sure I was going to have the mental, physical, emotional, and spiritual energy to show up how I needed to in order to give Mom the support she needed.

I expect that you are usually conscious of your physical energy levels. You know when you're a yawn-y disaster in the morning or mid-afternoon. You're aware of those days and times when you engage Potato Mode. And I bet you have some idea of how to manage your physical energy. Put away the devices before bedtime. Go to bed early. Get in some exercise. Drink lots of water. And so on.

But are you paying an equal amount of attention to managing mental, emotional, and spiritual energy levels? Are you clear about which activities help you recharge? And that sometimes you might need to exchange one type of energy for another?

Four Types of Energy

It's important to understand these different dimensions of your energy and how they work. Ignoring those nuances is like playing checkers but using chess pieces. Like...yes...you can do it...and it's workable, but you're missing some opportunities to level up your game.

Your mental energy is a measure of your available resources to spend on things like staying focused, problem solving, planning or exercising your willpower (no, no, I don't need to have another cookie... or wait...do I?). It's all front-brain activity.

Your emotional energy relates to how emotionally available you are in the present moment. Are you able to exercise self-awareness? Are you shut down or defensive? Are you numb? Are you feeling all the feelings? Maybe too many of them and too deeply?

Your spiritual energy reflects how truly yourself you're able to feel. Whether you derive your spirituality from an organized religion, a connection to a higher power, the people around you, nature, or some other source, it is the sense of peace, purpose, and rejuvenation you feel when you connect to something that's fully beyond you.

Your physical energy is the measure of how ready and able you feel to move through your day, functionally, doing all the things you need to do. It's your get up and go juice.

If you are physically exhausted, you may also feel like you have a foggy brain, or your willpower is low, or you're emotionally on edge, and so on. This is why it is important to appreciate the distinctions between them.

These energies are intertwined.

If you're not recharging yourself in one of the four types of energy but feel pretty good in the other three, you will feel okay, but you'll also know something is missing or feel off-balance. It's like an airplane that has lost power to one of its engines while at cruising altitude. The plane can still fly, but you better believe those pilots are paying close attention to the situation because while things are going okay, everything is not fine!

Figuring Out My Funk

I stumbled onto this phenomenon four-ish years ago. Keep in mind that I'm 42 as I write this. That's a long time to fly blind on something so fundamental. Yikes!

I was in a funk. Things were okay, but I was restless and unfulfilled in some way I couldn't identify. Things were good at home with Megan and at work. It was winter in Michigan. For many, it's a grim season. These are the folks who become "snowbirds" in later life. It's a weird term, I realize, because "snowbirds" want nothing to do with snow. They dash off to condos and cottages in Florida and Alabama and Texas shortly after the leaves have fallen.

Me? I like the snow. For two months. After that, it's time to giddy up to springtime. But snow is pretty and I enjoy the way a blizzard transforms the landscape. The funk settled into me well within the bounds of my two-month winter-and-snow grace period, so that wasn't the issue either.

I was talking with Brie during a coaching session about how things were going and admitted to the funk. I couldn't point to any-

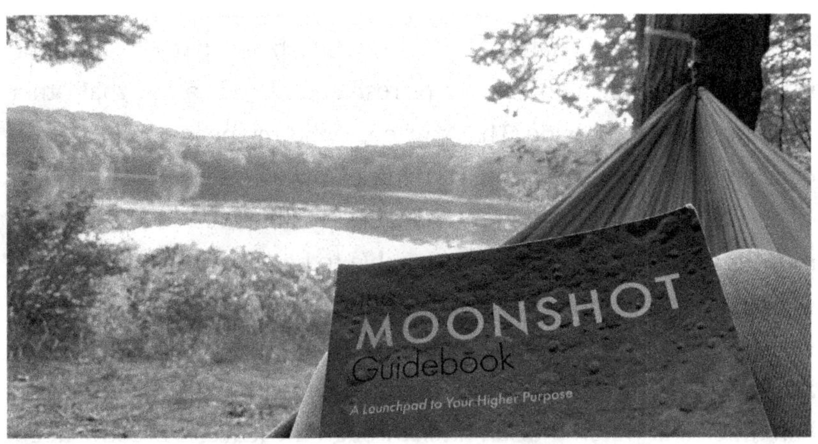

Visioning lakeside, on the North Country Trail

thing going badly, and there were plenty of things that were great, so why the funk?

Brie asked questions that got me thinking and soon we were onto something. In warmer months, I spend so much of my time outdoors playing disc golf, hanging out in my hammock reading a book, going for a hike, or working on some project around my property.

As we talked, we built a hypothesis that the funk was related to me not living fully during the winter months (an engine was out!), and that I needed to find ways to get outdoors even when it's frigid.

Meanwhile, coworkers had attended a conference where they learned a practice called MEPS and brought it back for us to try. At the beginning of the meeting, each participant describes their Mental, Emotional, Physical, and Spiritual landscape by choosing a different word (or at most a sentence) for each.

This got me thinking about what spirituality meant to me. I was raised in the Christian church, but over the years drifted away from that faith. In the absence of belonging to an organized religion, I didn't give any thought to my spiritual life. Welp, that was a mistake. I was running on "E" and didn't realize it.

As a result of that practice, I realized being out in nature, no matter the season, allows me to refresh and reset in a way that other activities do not provide. That's where I find my peace and what recharges me the most, minute by minute.

Making that connection changed my life. Even in the warmer months where I'm outside a lot, I'm able to be more intentional about creating mindful moments for myself where I can really soak in my surroundings. I go for quiet, meditative walks. I take a barefoot walk around my yard and feel all the textures beneath my feet. I lay in my hammock and watch the sun filter through the leaves. I breathe deep, especially when I'm out in the woods, taking in the loamy earth and leaves combined with the delicate smell of blossoming trees. I listen to birds, chipmunks, squirrels, crickets, and frogs all chirping and chattering away. I'm blissing out just typing this passage.

In the winter months, I now make it a point to go cross-country skiing when it's snowy out and go for hikes when it's not too snowy or bitter cold. I recognize that even the act of taking the dogs out for a short walk or shoveling snow gives me the opportunity to breathe deep and enjoy those moments where chores put me out in nature.

Becoming conscious of my deeper connection to nature has helped me find spiritual supplements for when the weather is unbearably cruddy. I've recognized that cooking, especially new recipes, is an excellent replacement for outdoor projects. The same parts of my brain light up in the process. It's a highly sensory experience. It allows me to act on my curiosity and learn. It brings me a sense of accomplishment and can involve problem-solving, just like my yard projects.

I wouldn't have noticed if I hadn't first keyed in on which outdoor experiences are the most fulfilling and exciting. Now I get to lean into that fully. I've prepared 51 new recipes so far this winter.

Because I've become aware of these aspects of my nature and what speaks to me from a deep, spiritual place, I have access to more

Me, bundled up for 15°F cross-country skiing

joy in my daily life. Even in Michigan in early March. Thanks, Brie!!

What about you? What do you do to recharge or reset when you find yourself in a funk? Are you clear on what type of energy is on "E" and how you can get back to good?

It's Not All Equal

Once you have your eye on the four types of energy, it's time to sort out what drains you, what refills you, and at what rates.

This will have so much to do with your personality type. Get ye to a personality test!

For example, I am a:

- S (DiSC)
- ISTJ-A (16 Personalities)
- Type Three (Enneagream)
- Achiever/Learner/Futuristic/Strategic/Input (Strengthsfinder)
- Honesty/Zest/Humor/Perseverance/Curiosity (ViaCharacter)

- Acts of Service/Words of Affirmation (top 2 Love Languages)
- Ravenclaw (Time Magazine and Buzzfeed Harry Potter Sorting Hat quizzes)

In chapter 1, I shared my revelation about my introverted work style and how it compliments and contrasts the strengths of my extroverted peers. That is why it behooves you to take personality tests. It will increase self-awareness of your strengths, shed light on your blind spots, and help you better understand how your teammates operate.

When it comes to energy, learning how you're built will give you insight into what motivates you (gives you energy) and what serves as a stressor (draining energy). I've spent the most time with DiSC, as it's part of the toolkit we use with our employees at the BIGGBY Home Office. It directly addresses the idea of stressors and motivators.

When you finish the DiSC assessment, you get a report covering the tendencies of people with your DiSC style and how to understand and work with folks with different styles. As an S style, I'm an even-keeled people person (and often a people pleaser) who thinks before speaking and is slow to act. In the report, the list of stressors and motivators includes things you'd expect with that kind of build. When I look at the list, most of them are true for me.

I love working with people who care about what we're doing and similarly, in my personal life, my closest relationships are with people who demonstrate care for others. I gain deep satisfaction from knowing I have made a difference, whether that's from providing direct support to someone or by creating something that others find useful.

Meanwhile, on the stressor side of the equation, there's people stuff there too. Saying "no" is difficult for me. Doesn't mean that I can't do it, but I usually try to find some way to say yes. Giving people critiques requires effort. People who act angry, pushy, or self-centered take a lot of energy out of me (which is one of the reasons I avoid most reality TV...that type of "drama" isn't entertaining—it's exhausting).

The trick when working with any personality test is that the results will never ever ever catch the full complexity of who you are as a person. Interrogate your test results to see what feels like absolute truth and what seems absurd when you try to map it onto your lived experience. It's also worth talking about your results with others in case they can see something in the results that you can't. It's possible the test is pointing to tendencies hidden in a blind spot. Asking others provides a reality check.

The Milksteamer's Moody Mirror

One stressor that is entirely missed in my DiSC results is that in addition to having an introverted work style, I'm also socially introverted. You've already read about my childhood experiences, so this might be easy to picture. I have more to say about my experiences as a social introvert, but for now, let's talk about how this relates to managing my energy levels.

My career path has helped (forced?) me to learn how to flip a switch and become outgoing. I hired into the company as a barista for a part-time summer job while attending Michigan State University. I recognized very quickly that the company was doing things differently. The first day of training introduced me to our operating philosophy: PERC. Each letter of the acronym represents a statement about the outcomes we're trying to achieve. The first three are all focused on the customer experience and C is focused on product quality.

R stands for "Recognize each customer as an individual," or as I later began to think of it: "Everyone deserves to feel special." One of our best opportunities is when our customers wait to pick up their drink. The barista responsible for finishing and serving the drink inside the store, the Milksteamer, is officially responsible for proactively engaging each customer in conversation.

Those interactions have built life-long levels of brand loyalty for our customers while also setting the stage for the second-favorite part of the job for our baristas—interacting with regulars.

It is also super effective for dragging shy-leaning baristas, kicking and screaming, out of their shells. I've heard countless baristas cite this as: A) A really uncomfortable part of getting started in the job, and B) A life skill that they're grateful for having had the chance to build.

That was me, for sure. While training, the first time I worked as the Milksteamer I had so much of my mental energy focused on making small talk with my customer that I turned on the steam wand before submerging it in the pitcher of milk. If you want to have a direct sense of my experience and you have a straw handy, get yourself a glass of water (or milk if you dare) and blow some bubbles. Fun, right? Yeah, that's the way it's supposed to work. If, instead, you want to try it the way I did it that afternoon, take the straw out of the water, start blowing hard through it, and gently bring it to the surface of the water. See the difference? Did it get a little...splattery? Now imagine ten times the force. It was a milk volcano aimed point-blank at my face. I didn't make that mistake again.

My struggle to learn the ropes of being a Milksteamer was made all the worse because the manager who hired me, Eric, was a 10 out of 10 natural extrovert. After going through training and getting some repetitions working on the quieter evening shift, I began to get scheduled to work next to Eric on the espresso machine while he worked as the Milksteamer.

I was in the "Shotpuller" position, doing this a couple hundred times a morning: read the drink ticket, add flavored syrups to the cups as needed, hand-tamp freshly ground espresso, lock the portafilter into the machine, press the double ristretto button, pour the beautiful silky shots into the cup, and then say "All set" so Eric could finish the drink with steamed milk, whipped cream, and so on.

Meanwhile, Eric wasn't just engaging his customer in conversation, he would have the entire lobby, full of waiting customers, engaged. Sort of like Mickey Mouse, as the sorcerer's apprentice in the movie *Fantasia*, commanding the attention and directing the fun of every customer in this ongoing, organic, flowing conversation, peppered throughout with his terrible Laffy Taffy-grade jokes. I was wildly intimidated by Eric's prowess.

With practice, I improved. Like all BIGGBY stores today, we have a trivia of the day board, an easy tool for me to lean on, asking the customer if they knew the answer. I ended up recognizing that would only buy me 10 or 15 seconds of interaction where I might need a full minute.

I learned to keep the focus on the customer. I learned to avoid questions like "What are you up to today?" because too often that led to clipped responses: "Ah, nothing," "Work" or "Shopping." Instead, I'd often ask "Where are you headed next?" The specificity of the question demonstrated that I had genuine interest in their answer. That question yielded answers with more meat to them: "Going home," "Headed to the job site" or "Shopping at the mall." Because the expectation was to keep the customer engaged during their entire wait for their drink, I couldn't just leave the conversation there, so I would ask follow-up questions. I learned to build the conversation.

What first intimidated me became my favorite position on the line. On a busy morning, I would have small conversations with no fewer than one hundred people. Sometimes as many as two hundred. That's five hundred to one thousand pieces of small talk in a working week. I was at the store for three years and worked many more busy mornings than slower nights. Adding it all up, I figure I led 40,000 small-talk conversations. I developed a life skill.

Store 3 barista days

At the same time, I developed an understanding about how energy gets shared between people. The barista training materials talked about how the Milksteamer is on stage, so leave your baggage at the door and project an air of happiness, no matter how you're feeling. That can feel like tough advice some days at the start of a shift.

Tough advice, but wise. The act of putting on a brave face and trying to be friendly even in the midst of a crappy day is the best shot you have to turn your mood around.

The energy we give out bounces back.

If I was terse or full of sighs throughout the course of my shift, I would receive that (and worse) back from customers. Picture this from the customer perspective or even from your own experience... how often have you walked away from an employee interaction thinking to yourself "Geez...what's their problem?"

If instead I did my very best to keep the focus squarely on that next customer, smiled as best as I could, and asked about them and their day, I earned myself a steady stream of smiling and kind interactions back from them. It became inevitable that at some point in the shift I would realize I'm actually having a good time here!

The energy I gave out bounced back to me. That meant on any given crummy day, I had the opportunity to choose—Do I stay in my feelings and keep me and my customers in a downward toilet bowl spiral or do I want to put my chin up and help us all climb out of the muck of my mood? As my grandma "Mimi" would say: "Make it a good day—you have the power."

I learned that I could flip a switch and project friendly outgoingness even when my default was to slink home to my bedroom and video games.

The Introvert at the 600-Person Party

That lesson—that I could flip a switch to change how I'm projecting myself—became one of my most-used tools across my first ten years at BIGGBY.

Over my years as the Director of Training, I was "on stage" countless times, training staff at our new store openings and groups of new franchisees, managers, and store trainers at our Training Center.

As the trainer, the whole show rests on you. You're the lead actor (and for that matter, the director, the set designer, the prop master, and craft services), and all eyes are on you. For a guy who is socially introverted, it was nerve-wracking, but I learned how to get by.

At the beginning of any of those trainings, I would serve drinks to people as they arrived, insisting that I work the line at the Milksteamer position. I don't think I was conscious of any of this at the time, but looking back, it was a brilliant plan. I got to slide into a well-known and comfortable role where the rules of engagement are clear.

I was able to introduce myself and break the ice with people one at a time before having to face the (intimidating) entire class.

I would always (and I cannot emphasize always enough) be nervous when I stepped in front of the class for the first time. I doubt they could see my nerves—the switch was flipped. My personality was ten times larger than in any social setting in my private life. I projected charming and outgoing confidence.

Internally, I was shaky. I learned the fastest way to shake off the nerves was to introduce myself by sharing who I am, what I do for the company, and what I do when I'm not BIGGBY-ing. It was natural to start off with an intro, but it also created a well-worn and safe runway to get me off the ground. I'd hand it over to each trainee to do a brief intro, and I would ask questions and riff with them. By the end of that ritual, I was settled in. I faked it 'til I made it.

By the end of the day, however, I felt a magnetic pull tugging at me to get out of that store so I could get back to my hotel room and my own agenda. That's a funny way of putting it...the whole day of training was also, quite literally, my agenda. And that's where a keen distinction lies—for me, it's not about being able to do the thing that I want to do that recharges me...it's that I can do what I want without having to worry about anyone else in the process.

This was an epiphany. I'm not an antisocial introvert. I love people. But they also make me tired. I'm not sure how much of this was in me before I started working at BIGGBY, but how I behave in group settings today is how I behaved all those years behind the counter. I focus on the people around me. I make sure everybody is doing well, paying attention to their experience. And all the while, I often suppress my own needs to make sure the people around me are getting what they want.

That's why, by the end of those days of training, I just needed to be by myself and do my own thing. It's the same reason why during our big annual franchise meetings that I will take a short break in my hotel room or a quiet corner of the convention center if my schedule allows for it. A good ten minutes of solitude can do wonders for me.

I think if the average person observed me operating at our annual meeting, they would swear I'm an extrovert. They wouldn't mistake me for a center-of-attention-party-animal extrovert either, but I wouldn't be labeled as shy by the average bystander.

Well of course they wouldn't! I have that switch flipped. It's easily the most tiring thing I do each year. It means navigating a sea of people, moving from event to event through the halls, making small talk and catching up with people I haven't seen in a while. Don't get me wrong, it's really really great. I've known some of these folks for 20 years and there are so many people walking those halls who I legitimately love. But.

It also feels like a social minefield. The thing that causes me the most anxiety is a phenomenon I've had to deal with all too often—bumping into someone who clearly knows and remembers me and I can't say the same. You know this feeling. "Heeeeeeeeeeey, you! How are you doing?!" This is usually the consequence of me doing frequent trainings with groups of people where, over the course of the class I'm able to build up a nice amount of rapport with people, but across hundreds of classes and thousands of people, it's easy for me to remember the face but blank on the name.

I've found a few things that help me manage my energy across those tiring days as well as how to recharge at the end of each day.

1. A Chill Room: When the venue and agenda afford me the opportunity, I recharge with a short break back in my hotel room. Shoes off, put on some quiet music or maybe the TV and have some solo time. Oh, and the room is literally chilly, with the thermostat cranked down.
2. A Routine Roomie: Most Home Office staff sleep two to a

hotel room to help us manage our costs for the expensive-to-put-on event, and it's always been Tony and me. I know what to expect from him, and he from me. It gives me the chance to decompress with my friend. If I had a different roommate each year, I would have the added stressor of having that unknown waiting at the end of the day.

3. An Extroverted Icebreaker: Whether it's Brie, Alisha, or one of my other outgoing friends, I always feel more comfortable following in their ubersocial wake. Like an icebreaker ship, they're built to lead the way into conversation.
4. 1-on-1 Connection: While it drains me to "work a room," some of my fondest annual meeting memories revolve around extended one-on-one conversations where I leave with a genuine sense of knowing them better than I did before the conversation, as well as getting a little recharge right in the middle of the event.
5. A Recovery Day: If I'm able, I'll schedule myself to be off the day or two after the event to get a full dose of Jeremy-doing-just-what-Jeremy-wants-to-do-for-himself. Farting around in the yard for a full day does wonders for my ability to bounce back and be social again.

If you get clear on the things that drain and provide energy (physical, mental, emotional, and spiritual) you'll have the chance to be strategic about how you spend your time. You'll know what you need to refill your tank when you're running on empty. You'll find ways to keep yourself motivated in spite of the stressors that work against you. Self-knowledge always goes a long way!

Get in Motion: Understanding Your Energy

This may be the easiest activity in the whole book for you. Or you might find yourself staring hard at one or two of these questions, wondering which way is up. Ready?

Finding Your Motivators:

1. When you feel your very best – mentally, emotionally, physically, and spiritually—what has gotten you feeling that way? The activity itself, people you were with, the setting, the end result, something else or a combination of factors?
2. What activities can lead to you losing track of time, where you get into the zone? Are there themes in common to each activity you listed?
3. What activities did you enjoy as a child that you still enjoy today? Why?
4. If you're working on a project for a while, what factors help you keep going and do your best work? Is it a sense of accomplishment...checking things off the list? Is it the feeling of working alone or with a team? Is it the positive feedback that you hope to get about your work? Is it about leaving a mark, being known for what you've done? Something else?
5. When you've had a rough week, what is the best way you can spend the weekend in order to feel recharged for the following Monday?
6. Review what you've written for 1-5, then complete these statements:

- I am energized by...
- I feel great when...
- I find a sense of peace when...

Finding Your Stressors:

1. What in your life frustrates you? What activities do you wish you could hand off forever?
2. What types of interactions give you a sense of anxiety or dread, even with close friends or family?
3. What types of tasks are do-able but tiresome for you?
4. When working with a team, what frustrates you the most?
5. Describe a tough—but not traumatic—day. What makes for a hard day for you?
6. Review what you've written for 1-5, then complete these statements:

- I am worn out by...
- I feel down when...
- I find a sense of pressure or anxiety when...

Section Two

How's Your Vision?

Mom told me a story about one afternoon, when I was in preschool, how she came to the school to pick me up and my teacher called her aside for a conversation. She told Mom, "Either Jeremy is very stupid, or he needs glasses."

She told Mom that while playing a game where she would hold up different pictures to get the kids to say what the picture was, I identified a house as an apple, a bird as a hat, and a car as a candy bar.

Turns out that I was very nearsighted, taking after my mom. My brother would turn out to have 20-20 vision like my dad. Harumph.

Mom told me what it was like to watch me walk outside for the first time after being outfitted with my very first pair of glasses. That I gaped, mouth slack, eyes wide, taking in all of that detail. That I was particularly fascinated by the leaves on the trees.

It makes sense. I would have known the details of my parents' faces, my books, my stuffed animals—I would have held them all up close. But trees would have been indistinct green blobs.

Just imagine the before and after of that moment for four-year-old Jeremy. I had NO idea there was so much extra detail in the world around me. If I would have looked in the mirror, my own face would be indistinct.

Five years old with glasses that weighed six pounds

How clearly do you see yourself and the world around you? How would you even know if you had it all wrong?

Your self-perception affects your capability.

It changes what you think is possible, both in how you carry yourself and what you can achieve.

Getting feedback on how others see you is like the eye doctor clicking different lenses in front of you, asking which one is better. A or B? B or C? As you get more perspective, you get closer to clarity.

And that clarity will empower you.

You'll see how many more options you have in how you can be as a person, and adjust when necessary to get better results. You'll see the ways that your self-talk reinforces belief. You'll see how much freedom is possible when you live into those qualities that make you unique.

I'm excited for what you're going to discover. And regardless, I won't tell your mom that you're stupid.

VISION

Chapter Seven

Ways of Being

I have a hunch that you, my friend, have a control panel on your personality with a bunch of dials. Chances are you've fiddled with the dials consciously. For example, I'm guessing that when you were at a job interview, you intentionally tweaked some of your settings for that environment. The Pay Attention to Your Words dial was maxed out. The Be Self Conscious About Your Posture one got twisted up since the morning when you were scrolling social media. The Talk About Your Politics and Relationships dials were probably set a lot lower than when you were last among your close friends.

In a setting as formal as a job interview, you likely pay close attention to all of the settings that you are aware of. There are more dials than you know about, it's true. And until you find them, they're turned to your factory presets, for better and for worse.

We'll deal with that discovery process later – for now, let's just concern ourselves with the settings you already know you can control.

Your Presets

In the same way the average car stereo has presets for how much the bass, treble, and midrange are emphasized, our brains have developed presets for all those dials on our personality—even the ones we aren't conscious of.

Some function like factory presets. They're a part of your build, based on that special combination of nature, nurture, and life experience that has made you into you. Your settings will look different from mine, and from everyone else, for that matter, though some of the presets will share the same names. Home. Work. Friends. Family. School. Church.

I was conscious, growing up, of how I flipped between different settings as a part of the package deal that came with having divorced parents. Also included: missing lots of parties thrown by friends on the weekend, having eight grandparents, and getting to celebrate Christmas with two stockings.

Dad was strict compared to Mom. I could play things a bit looser with her. Things like listening to music like Pearl Jam or the Smashing Pumpkins, both of which I felt would get me in trouble with Dad. Watching an occasional R-rated movie (so long as it wasn't, you know, too R-rated), and if I let a swear word loose when I stubbed a toe, I wouldn't get in trouble with Mom for the slip.

So when I was at Dad's, there was a stronger filter setting engaged for my mouth and behavior. I wonder how much of that contributed to my introverted work style, where I tend to think a lot about the words I use before speaking them.

Meanwhile, when I was a teenager hanging out with friends, you can bet the Raunchy-and-Gross-Teenage-Boy dial was turned up to 11, saying the kind of things that make me grateful that I reached adulthood before smartphones and social media were a thing.

Those teenage years of just looking to fit in and get along were a crucial part of me stumbling around in life and unintentionally picking up a lot of the pieces that make me who I am.

Even as a kid, I understood, without having to think about it, that I could choose how I wanted to be. If you asked me back then, I might have described one of those versions as my "true" self. I probably would have said it was the version of me where I was hanging out with my friends, and the others (with Mom, with Dad, at church, at school, etc.) were like putting on masks to better fit in with those surroundings.

Today, I know that those were all me. It's me, choosing how to be. Adjusting dials.

The more aware you are of your presets and knowing which dials you can tweak, the more versatile you will become!

I move dials to better fit my situation. When giving a presentation, I use more formal language (no, not dressing up "who" as "whom," more like enunciating ends of words instead of my Midwestern "gonna" and "whatcha" style of speech) and I watch my mouth so I'm not casually swearing. When I'm with the people I'm closest to, I speak my mind without preamble—no repackaging my thoughts inside extra words to make sure my intent isn't mistaken. When I'm with mere acquaintances or strangers, my word filters get dialed up so I don't accidentally offend anyone.

Regardless of how my dials are set, it's all me. None of those presets are "truly me." I'm choosing how I want to be, based on my environment. Letting my swear words fly or whom-ing my way through a presentation is a choice that I get to make. Yeah, I fibbed earlier. I sneak a "whom" in now and then when no one is looking.

There are so many dials we get to tweak, if we're being conscious of them...Warm and Fuzzy or Direct and to the Point, Casual or Formal, Animated or Chill, Engaged or Removed, Loving or Cold, Self-Centered or Other-Focused, Adventurous or Timid, and on and on.

It's cool to just go with your presets and not worry about dial settings if that gets you where you want to go. If they help you be at your best with the people around you. If it doesn't do unintended damage.

How Can I Be for You Today?

It is in recognition of those dials that we coaches on the LifeLab team might open our sessions with a question that is specifically about adjusting our dials: "How can I be for you today?" This is important because as a coach, I start out every conversation with my I-Am-A-Coach preset engaged, or for coaching relationships that are well-established, I might have my Standard-Caitlin, Default-Chelsea or Normal-John presets clicked into place. The trick, however, is that on any given day, my standard I-Am-A-Coach preset (or even those customized presets for an individual) will be the exact wrong way of being that my coachee needs that day.

My most poignant lesson I've had on this didn't happen at work. It happened at the dinner table, long before I became a coach. Megan and I were sitting down to dinner and she was describing the bad day she'd had a work. I don't remember the meal we had, I don't remember what happened for Megan that made the day bad, or what I said to her, but I do remember how the conversation ended: Megan even more upset than at the beginning of the conversation, but now I was the cause. "I don't need you to solve my problem, I need you to listen and to be on my side!"

Got it. My dials were set wrong. She didn't need default Problem-Solving-Jeremy. She needed Empathetic-Husband-Jeremy. My natural tendency was wrong for that moment and I didn't know any better. If I would have asked "How can I be for you as we're talking?" I could have been a better husband to Megan that night.

We rarely think about our ways of being—about where all our dials are set—while we're in the moment with another person. We might look back on an interaction and think "Oooooof. I was a jerk." Or "Hey! Look at me go! That woulda made my mom proud just then!" Or "Ugh. That was not my best moment as a husband. Crap."

So while the question has a certain awkwardness to it, when it works, it works magic.

I've seen that magic on both ends of the question. In my sessions where Brie is coaching me, my frequent ask is that she helps to keep the conversation focused on me, where I'm at, what I can do, how I'm struggling, and so on. If we're not careful, it's easy for Brie and I to fall into territory where it's more like hanging out and brainstorming. We're friends and colleagues and we're both great at batting the conversational ball around. But in a coaching session, we need to keep the spotlight on me and what my opportunities are for growth, rather than just talking about what we're up to at work or home.

Many of my coachees answer the question "How can I be for you today?" by saying some version of "I'm not sure" or "Just be yourself." Those will always be the easiest answers for a coachee. They require no forethought or self-awareness.

When a coachee does lean in and expresses a need it's always helpful. I've heard things like: "I just need to vent...it will be okay, and I know I'll sort it out, but right now I'm just angry," "I'm feeling a little fragile right now, please don't push or challenge me, I'm not ready for that," or "Watch out for me in case I come across as playing the victim – that's my natural defense mechanism, and I'm trying to work on it."

That tells me exactly how I should set my dials, whether that's turning down natural instincts like problem-solving, challenging perspective, pushing for action, or turning up my sensitivity to a certain behavior.

We can choose how we want to be. Based on the setting or people, we get to choose.

This includes being able to choose to overcome the parts of our natural personality that hold us back. I don't want to be the short-tempered version of myself, sniping back when I feel attacked. I want to keep my head and respond with compassion so the conversation can become productive, rather than destructive.

Patrick, My Emotional Role Model

Earlier today, Alisha sent a gif in our team chat of Alexis Rose from the show *Schitt's Creek*, pulled from a scene where she's cheering on Stevie, saying "I got your back today, girl." Alisha added: "I am always channeling Alexis energy - I need you all to know that." And she does. Alisha is the cheerleader in my life. She radiates positivity, is an unparalleled hype girl, and is solidly on my side--even when she disagrees with me she still manages to signal that she's on my side. It's a superpower!

Which made me think—which *Schitt's* character would I like to channel? It didn't take long. Patrick. Absolutely Patrick. I admire him for being able to respond to nuclear-weapon-grade insecurity and emotional spinouts with bemused composure.

There's a scene where he wakes up to find that his fully grown adult fiancé has had a nighttime oopsie--wetting the bed they share. Here Patrick is, waking to find himself wet with urine and he manages to keep his head and talk his fiancé out of death-by-embarrassment. I think I already have parts of Patrick's demeanor but aspire to the emotional intelligence superpowers he displays from one episode to the next.

When I consider my default ways of being and how I want to replace some of the less productive ones, having a clear idea of who my emotional role models are helps me to better visualize my personal possibilities.

Who would you choose as your emotional role model?

Get in Motion: Identifying Your Ways of Being

Introspection Time! Get out some paper, your favorite note-taking app, or grab a friend to talk this out. Let's answer questions to pinpoint your presets and your "ways of being" goals!

What do you think about and how do you behave when you're...

1. At home?
2. At work?
3. With friends?
4. With family?
5. At a party?
6. In class?

How do you behave when you are...

7. Happy?
8. Afraid?
9. Lonely?
10. Fully present?

Your emotional role model

11. Which of your presets and personality dials do you wish you could change or have better control over?
12. Based on the above, how would you describe your emotional role model?

Chapter Eight

How Do I Be Me?

I don't know how many teenagers ask themselves, "How do I be me?" but I'm guessing it's not too many. I know I wouldn't have thought it when I was a teen. And yet...I and nearly every teenager who ever graced this earth with their hormone-addled presence spent a lot of time working through that problem.

I suppose every high school had a handful of kids who were non-conformist who bore the mark of "that's the weird kid," shunned by passing herds of teens rushing to buy their faddish clothing from the same store.

Bless the weirdos. They swam against the currents of popular culture despite how the typical teenage brain matures. For most of us, it's the way that our brains are physically developing that makes us so keyed-in on what others think.

It's like the *Extreme Home Makeover* bus pulls in front of the teenage prefrontal cortex. Walls are coming down, we've got new and better equipment going into the utility room and a brand-new kitchen perfect for hosting company. For a while, it's going to be a mess in there. Decision-making gets wonky. Risk assessment is a disaster. The ability to empathize by putting themselves inside others' perspectives increases dramatically. Meanwhile, glands in their bodies are shooting hormones into their bloodstream like water out of a firehose.

It's the perfect condition for the teenager in question to spend a lot of time thinking thoughts like: "Why doesn't anyone like me? Oh, I know, it's because (insert horrible self-talk here). Maybe if I (did that thing, dressed that way, behaved just so, etc.) they'd like me more!"

It's that combination of brain chemistry and thought process that leads teens to swerve hard into trying to fit in with hopes of being popular, according to whatever the current influencers are marketing to the teenage demographic.

Meanwhile, as we progress through our teenage years, we start spending more time outside the company of our parents and instead with our peers. That burgeoning independence creates space for forming our own identity, separate from who we were as children to our parents.

Is it any wonder that teenagers are so angsty? Their brains are getting overhauled, they're drenched in hormones, and suddenly they're out mixing it up in the world, trying to figure out who they are and where they belong.

It Takes a Village (of Nerds): Jeremy Finds a Place to Belong

I remember feeling bursts of newborn independence in my teenage years, particularly once I was able to drive and had my first job at a movie theater on the east side of Kalamazoo. Suddenly I was carving out my own little corner of life, away from my parents and the rest of my world. I was 16-years-old, working alongside kids who were my age, but also 20- and 30-somethings.

I enjoyed being my own person and being treated like an adult. I gained responsibility and earned respect. Plus, every now and then during summer vacation, I was able to convince my parents to let me stay out late to watch an employee-only screening of one of the movies being released the following day, while treating ourselves to mildly stale popcorn served out of giant (unused) trash bags. It was a fun gig.

But while I enjoyed that sense of independence, I don't have any memory of intentionally exploring who I was as my own person. That would wait until I landed in college.

I attended Michigan State University, only an hour away from home, but in a lot of ways it felt like the other side of the world. Only three other people from my graduating class went to MSU, all of whom I was friendly with, but spread out across the large campus, we rarely saw each other.

So there I was, living away from my parents for the first time and in a population that was 99.99999 percent strangers. When applying for MSU, I also chose to apply for Lyman Briggs, a sort of school-within-a-school at Michigan State for students interested in science majors. I was interested in Lyman Briggs because I enjoyed my high school science classes and was thinking about becoming a high school science teacher as a career. The biggest appeal of getting into Lyman Briggs was their students predominately all live in the same dormitory building. This meant that I would be living with many of the people who were in class with me. It was a way for me to get that familiar small-town school vibe that I grew up with despite attending a college with more than 40,000 students.

I also applied to the Honors College at MSU. Upon being accepted, I decided to live on the Honors floor of the dorm, with more than a couple nudges from my parents. I suspect that was following the line of logic that if I'm with a bunch of other kids who got straight A's in high school that I wouldn't be as likely to keg stand my way through my college career.

The net effect of those choices ended up being great for me in a lot of ways. Unlike high school, where I largely felt like a sore thumb always sticking out in the broader culture, I found a place of belonging in that dorm. In high school, I felt like I should be embarrassed about being a good student – that was the message I got from being bullied and from other snide comments across the years. My friends didn't treat me that way, but walking those halls in gen pop I never felt comfortable just being me.

At MSU, I never felt like I was wrong for studying, and for trying hard, and for being interested in learning. It was just natural to let that part of myself be free. Meanwhile, living on that floor with maybe 100 other people from all over the place, it was like a little village. The floor was divided in half by an elevator lobby, with the guy's rooms on one side and the women's rooms on the other. Many people left their doors open when they were hanging out in their rooms, giving the floor a casual social nature, making it easy to say hello and check in and chat with people as you walk by. In the afternoon and evening, after most people were done with class, the sounds of dozens of different types of music, TV shows, and video games would mingle from one end of the hallway to the other.

I stayed up late in those days, hanging out or studying, depending on which night of the week it was and how close I was to an impending due date or exam day. Those countless late-night hours featured so many wandering and occasionally deep conversations.

Because of the free-wheeling casually social nature of the floor, the people involved in the conversations would be a different group of people from one night to the next, based on who was able to hang out or who was trying to focus by working in the "study hall" room that adjoined the elevator lobby. This was important, because while I had a core group of friends on the floor who I was closer with, you'd always have a sprinkling of other perspectives getting mixed in.

And everyone was in roughly the same boat, too. No matter where we came from, we were all trying to figure out our lives while under the pressure of our classes, away from our parents and families. I think the pressure of our classes created a lower-key but similar type of environment for bonding to what you see amongst soldiers—we came to rely on one another to get through. Whether that was emotional support or help trying to learn the content of the classes we shared, we built trust along the way. It was a safe environment for people to wrestle with the big things in life – politics, religion, sexuality, philosophy, fears, and ambition. For my part, across my first couple years in college, I came away with some big lessons about who I was and who I wanted to be.

The Lessons My Classes Taught Me About Me

I attended a class about Christianity, which explored the history of the religion and just how political it all was, including the creation of the Bible itself, planting seeds of disillusionment that wouldn't sprout until years later. In the meantime, I became less interested in going to church. That was a non-negotiable back home with Dad, but away from home I could choose to go or not to go. I went to a few different local churches with different friends across the first couple years at MSU. Nothing stuck and it was my choice how I would spend my Saturday nights and/or Sunday mornings now.

I learned that I wasn't as good a college student as I was a high school student. A combination of factors led to this. A four-day-a-week 8:00 AM calculus class may have been the tipping point on that one. Side note: Dear reader, if you are a high school student preparing to go to college and you go to orientation at the college where some other slightly older college kid helps give you advice on which classes you should take, please be careful and don't listen to everything they say.

The short version of the story of me learning about myself as a student was: I discovered skipping class. I never did that in high school. Not ever. But in college? Sometimes 8:00 am was just too early to be sitting under the fluorescent lights, being overwhelmed by how much I didn't actually know about the subject for which my high school teacher, a very nice woman, but maybe not the best calculus teacher, gave me an A. My college calculus professor gave me a 2.5. That's a C+. Yikes.

By the end of my freshman year, I had learned that I was not going to be a science teacher. I struggled in my chemistry class as well as my honors cell and molecular biology class. I toiled to follow the professors during their lectures and the bookwork didn't go much better for me. Two more 2.5s. The high school valedictorian was on the cusp of slipping below a 3.0. Cue a mild identity crisis. Can a crisis be mild? I suppose not. Let's try this instead: cue an identity dilemma.

I ended up deciding to switch to an English major, still thinking that I would become a high school teacher. I was a life-long reader and had done well with writing assignments in high school, making it a natural choice. That choice left me back and swimming in a sea of strangers for my classes, however, as I would no longer be going to class with all my friends and floor-mates. I was now one of only a small handful of people on my floor who had non-science majors.

My grades turned right around, with a string of 4.0 English classes, up until I ran into the brick wall that was the required English Literature from 1660 to 1789 class...why, hello 2.5, I haven't seen you in a while!

Aside from that and another dreadful literature class, the going got easier for me. I had to finish out a few science classes to be able to repurpose those freshman year credits into a science minor. Microbiology was brutal because I just didn't have the building blocks for the course work in my brain, but I just needed to pass, and pass I did – a bruising but workable 1.5.

Looking back on it, the struggle I had in my freshman year as well as during an episode at work that you'll read about in chapter 11, I have taken away this lesson: "it shouldn't be this hard."

I do not mean: "life cannot be difficult" or "I should never struggle" or "avoid challenge at all costs." When I say "it shouldn't be this hard" I am painting the difference between a person swimming hard through choppy water versus a person who doesn't know how to swim flailing around, on their way to drowning.

If you are living your life feeling like you are just, barely, keeping your head above water, and are just...so...tired, that is what I'm talking about. It's an awful feeling, not just because of the struggle, but because you're struggling AND you can't see the shore from where you are.

When I changed majors, even though there were plenty of challenges to those English classes—assignments that stretched me beyond my initial capability or required me to pour hours and hours of time into reading and writing, I understood the contour of the challenges. I had a sense of direction and knew that I could fight my way through it. I was no longer drowning.

You in All of Your Glorious You-ness

BIGGBY has a set of values it has identified that we refer to as the cultural values of the company: Have Fun, Make Friends, B Yourself, and Share Great Coffee. We promote these values publicly because doing so attracts the "right" kind of people to the brand, as customers, employees, and franchise owners. We think that if people see those words and think, "ooh, yep, I like that," then they're likely to have the sorts of other traits that would make them a good fit, likely to stick around, do the right thing, and so on.

This is the second iteration of those values, changed from the original and fairly similar list of: B Happy, Have Fun, Make Friends, Love People, and Drink Great Coffee. It's not that we don't want our people to be happy, of course, but that we were more interested in strongly declaring that we want you to just be you, and that we'll love you for it. We don't want you to fake being somebody else or keep other parts of your life locked away and hidden when you're at work. Plus, if you're sharing great coffee, having fun, making friends, all while being yourself, we think it's likely you'll be happy as a natural side effect.

I love that we have that stated value:

Be Yourself.

I wish we could embrace it as an entire culture, not just at BIGGBY, but as a nation. Living in a culture that wants you to be yourself means that unconditional love is present – you don't have to put on airs to fit in here, we want you to be your true self and we'll love you for it!

So much harm is caused across the world where people feel forced to live a lie. It happens in so many settings...employees who have to live outside of their personal values when they're at work in order to keep bringing home a paycheck or in order to move up inside the organization. It also feeds the dynamic of people professing one thing when they're in the pew at church but living differently the other six days of the week. It happens inside families when one of the kids or dad or mom chooses to stay in the closet to avoid upsetting the rest of the family.

Thinking about the mental and emotional anguish it causes people to stay closeted with their family, friends, or coworkers reminds me of advice that I heard Dan Savage repeatedly offer to callers in that situation on his podcast Savage Lovecast. He would advise them that coming out becomes a superpower—that it will tell you who your true friends and family are. That if a person in their life chooses to reject them because they are gay (or any other stripe in the queer rainbow) then they don't deserve to be your friend.

I wouldn't, and I doubt that Dan would, discount just how painful it could be to have someone who is so close to you reject you, but that does not compare to the day-to-day pain of living a lie. Not to mention that rejection is the worst-case scenario, but things could also turn out best-case or anywhere else in between!

Imagine being able to live your truth and being celebrated for it by the people in your life!

And these examples have all been based upon the hugely important aspect of one's sexual orientation or gender identity—these are very high-stakes examples! But the dynamic plays out the same no matter what example we use, just to appropriately varying degrees.

Let's turn our focus to something that is both lower stakes and also within my lived experience.

I have only found more happiness in my life and my career the more I am able to bring my full and true self forward. One of the ways I've experienced this is by bringing together parts of my personal life and my work life, and the people who inhabit those separate worlds, together.

This topic reminds me a lot of the friendship that I struck up with Jon, a one-time franchisee with BIGGBY who I got to know better through that first Leadership Forum that we launched. If we stuck to surface-level stuff, I'm not sure if I would have had the chance to become close friends with Jon. He's close to 10 years younger than me, and a dad of three.

But the Forum provided an opportunity for all its members to share the surface-y fun details along with our deeper joys, pain, and dreams, it created a lot of opportunity for connection. In fact, there were numerous friendships born out of the connections made in each Forum we've launched.

Jon and I ended up bonding over a mutual love of fantasy novels, board games, and beer. We've remained close since he sold his stores, and I regard him as one of my best friends. He lives in the Grand Rapids area, which has afforded us the opportunity to get together over the years. I love catching up about life and sharing our thoughts about the latest Brandon Sanderson novel at one of our favorite breweries or playing board games with our other friends at one of our houses.

This entire friendship owes itself to us taking the opportunity—at work—to show up as our full brewery-book-and-boardgame-loving selves.

Every time you show up in all your glorious you-ness, you will shine brighter and brighter in your life.

True brilliance will never be found through imitation. The moon, pretty as it can be, and stimulating as it is for werewolves and tides, will never shine as bright as the sun itself.

I know that the further I have been able to lean into my me-ness, the happier and more productive I have been. Just think: How do you show up to jobs, tasks, or events that you're looking forward to and enjoy doing? How much more light and energy and productivity do you bring into those moments, contrasted with the times where you go in, dragging your feet, sighing, and wondering how long until it's over? Like night and day, no?

Realign things in your life to complement your you-ness—whether that's things in your physical space, your work, or the way you spend your downtime. Start showing up and shining as only you can do!

P.S. Opinions Are Like...You Know

One more reason to just be yourself and forget what other people think or have to say: Opinions are based on a person's perspective and have zero validity beyond the boundaries of that person's brainpan.

I love fresh pico de gallo. Chunks of tomato, onion, and spicy peppers laced with insanely addictive cilantro? Nom, nom, nom, nom. My wife? More like nope, nope, nope, nope. She can't deal with chunks of tomato or onion (though she doesn't object to the flavors), she's a self-proclaimed wimp about spicy food, and is one of those poor humans who think that cilantro tastes like soap.

Which one of us is right about pico de gallo? You might have your own individual feelings and choose to side with one of us, but of course the answer is: both of us, for ourselves, and neither of us for each other! So long as I'm not force-feeding Megan pico de gallo and so long as she doesn't mind me having some on the table for taco night, everybody wins!

And that's just pico de gallo!

I have a thousand opinions. You'll agree with some of them and you'll hate some of the others. Ready to play along? Here's a sampler platter:

1. Eggs? Sunnyside up. Bacon? Crispy. Toast? With creamy peanut butter. Breakfast for dinner? Nope.
2. The Godfather is superior to Godfather II.
3. College basketball > college football > NFL > (all of the other televised sports) > golf.
4. Beyonce is fine.
5. Star Wars is more fun than Star Trek.
6. If you don't listen to a little bit of music every day, you're doing it wrong.
7. IPAs are lovely but 99 percent of hazy IPAs are cloying and

gross.

8. Being outdoors is better than being indoors.
9. Skydiving looks fun.
10. If your pet doesn't have any fur, it's not a pet, it's a creature.

How are we doing? Did you go 10 for 10 agreeing with me? Think you could go 100/100? Or 1,000/1,000? I'm guessing not.

This is why trying to live your life based on the opinions of others is a forever-losing game. There is no perfect intersection where everyone agrees. So just be you! It takes less energy, makes you happier, and will bring your brilliance to bear on the rest of the world!

Get in Motion: Showing Up as Your Full True Self

There is so much beauty and power waiting for you when you start to live as your full and brilliant self. Let's do some thinking around what it could take for you to get there, if you aren't already! Time for some more journaling or talking things through with a good friend!

1. Where and with whom do you feel like you can be yourself? Why?
2. Where and with whom do you feel like you cannot be yourself? Why?
3. What is the very worst that could happen if you did show up as your full and authentic self in the places and with the people you listed for #2?
4. What's the best that could happen?
5. What's a middle-ground example of what could happen?
6. What do you think is the most likely?
7. Given how you've answered, are there spaces in your life

where it might be worth showing up in a way where you're living your truth? What would be a small way to try this?

I hope you can step more fully into your truth in your life. It might or might not go the best-case scenario route, but even if it doesn't, remember what Dan Savage said about your superpower and how pointless it is to try to live for the sake of someone else's opinion of you!

Chapter Nine

Self-Perception is NOT Reality

My whole life I have been fat. At least that's what I thought. Then one day, as a 38-year-old, I stumbled across my high school yearbook photo from my senior year. "What the crap?! I wasn't fat at all!" But if you would have asked me to describe myself as a school kid I would have said "pudgy" or perhaps I might have dredged up the trauma of shopping for jeans with my mom and use the term "husky."

Husky?! What the crap! They still use that term, I see. Just Googled it, expecting to see an article about how "husky" was relegated to the catalog of shameful terminology that was widely used in movies and TV of the less-enlightened years of the eighties and nineties. Nope. Searching it today brought up listings for Walmart, Target and others, where that's still an official size for children's clothes. What are we doing, people?

The fashion industry (and more pointedly, its marketing) is responsible for so much shame in our collective psyche, and their sins go well beyond narrow-minded naming for kids sizes. Many people carry around a warped self-image that can easily be traced back to the ways our subconscious absorbed the messages of all of those ads; or in this specific case, me thinking that I was husky because my jeans said so.

But here's the thing—I wasn't. Looking back at pictures of me from my childhood and teenage years I cannot fathom how that poor kid walked around carrying the burden of that kind of thinking.

And yet. That was the story that I'd written for myself. I was wrong. That wasn't my first or only epiphany about how messed up my self-perception is, especially on the topic of body image.

I had another lightning-bolt moment the year before that. I was out to dinner with some work friends and one of them was running himself down for the way he looked, every bit as negative in his self-talk as I was with mine. Here's the thing: This guy is literally a male model. Physically beautiful in all the ways we've been raised to think of beauty.

Just like we write stories about how the world around us works, we also write stories about ourselves.

I just looked at him completely dumbfounded. That was when the lightning bolt struck: It doesn't matter how symmetrical your features are or what your body mass index is...we're all struggling inside the four walls of our headspace.

Our self-perception is a function of our subconscious. Our whole lives it's just been recording data points and stringing them together to make stories.

As a kid, my subconscious was likely scribbling notes about "husky" size jeans, Mom buying diet food like rice cakes, and Dad getting us the McLean Deluxe in the McDonald's drive-thru, as well as all the images that media would have imprinted on the back wall of my brain.

I'm sure that there are plenty of other data points my subconscious filed away, but they're feeling undetectable now as I try to look back and guess what they could be. Visible or not, they were there, and they added up to form a narrative that I was a chunky kid. So I lived my life accordingly.

We live inside our stories.

That story went into a chapter book of stories whose moral is: Be shy, avoid the spotlight, be wary of the people who are popular, invest yourself in other areas of life than the physical--don't do sports, don't dance, don't sing or do karaoke (all of that despite being objectively well-coordinated and with a voice that can carry a tune). Those were the self-limiting beliefs that my subconscious chiseled into the granite of my personality.

The good news: I've learned a lot about how messed up my self-perception is, which has created the opportunity for me to do some overhauls on the way that I see myself. We'll deal with the self-talk portion of what I've learned in the next chapter and for now we'll focus on what it takes to get a clearer perspective on ourselves and what we have to offer the world.

You Are NOT Here

My happy place is deep out in the woods, on a day hike with my camping hammock, a good book, and maybe a beer tucked into my backpack. I don't bring a compass out with me because I have my phone on me, and even if service is spotty out there, I have a pretty solid sense of direction outdoors.

Megan hates being outdoors. Or more specifically, Megan hates the bugs that are outdoors. Oh, and apparently all forms of pollen have sworn a blood oath against her. Come to think of it, I'm lucky that she's willing to share the responsibility of taking out the dogs to do their business.

Meanwhile, Megan is an awfully good shopper, as well as an excellent finder of things. No sense of direction out in the world, but inside a mall? Even though we rarely make it to the mall these days, she has a never-fail ability to orient. I, on the other hand, lose whatever innate ability I have the second I step inside those doors. I also immediately forget where I've parked, but that's another story.

Because of this, especially back in the days when my Christmas shopping would have almost entirely happened inside of a mall, I was completely reliant upon those store directory maps they have near the entrances—it's the only way I knew where I was or where I wanted to go.

I should mention that I don't especially enjoy the act of shopping...I'd much rather be able to drop in like a Navy SEAL team, quickly and efficiently accomplish my mission, and then airlift out at top speed. All the more reason why I'd rely on those maps. Find my stores, plan a route, bing bang boom, I'm out of there.

Imagine, however, if the map was wrong. If the "You Are Here" star was misplaced. Or the stores were labeled incorrectly in the directory. What's the outcome there? My route would look more like one of those ambling paths the kid in the old Family Circus comic strip took around his neighborhood...a dotted line twisting and turning, doubling back on itself. Great for a step count if you're going for that, but if, like me, you're looking for Navy SEAL-precision, all it means is I'd be a few hundred more steps away from a full-on grown man temper tantrum.

I've got some bad news for you. Most of us are walking through life with an equivalently terrible map that we're relying on.

Many of us have a completely warped perspective of who we are and what we're capable of accomplishing in life.

We pick up these limiting self-beliefs along our path through life like a ship slowly becoming overcome by barnacles.

If we're going to live our best lives, it's going to mean finding those crusty little suckers and scraping them off. But it's more than that- part of the process is going to involve replacing them with something a lot more empowering. So, in our metaphor, that means we're going to bedazzle the hull? Paint it in camouflage? Graffiti affirmations?

We Take What We Know for Granted

I am about to give you a pep talk. You might need to brace yourself. I am grabbing you on both sides of your head, gently but firmly, and tilting your head so I can look you straight in the eyes when I say this to you:

YOU ARE COMPLETELY WHOLE AND PERFECT! YOU AS YOU ARE NOW. YOU ARE WORTHY OF LOVE. YOU ARE WORTHY OF RESPECT. YOU CARRY A GIFT THAT IS UNIQUE: YOUR YOU-NESS.

One of the most subtly awesome and simultaneously nasty tricks that we're capable of as humans is to accumulate all kinds of knowledge across our life in a way that is unintended. Those accumulated experiences help to form our unique perspective. Here's the nasty part: Because it can happen unintentionally, even effortlessly, we take our knowledge and the power of our perspective completely for granted.

I got clear on this because of Microsoft Excel.

My foot-in-the-door position at the BIGGBY Home Office was doing data entry part-time. This was in the years before every retailer you know had online customer reward and loyalty programs. At BIGG-BY, like many other stores of that era, we had a paper loyalty card that our frequent customers would carry. They'd buy a beverage and we'd give them an ink "B" stamp, and after 12 stamps they earned a free beverage.

Yes, paper. Yes, an ink stamp. Yes, it feels old-timey, not very far removed from dripping candle wax onto an envelope to press it closed with your personal seal. Anyway, on the back side of this yes-teryear stamp card were spaces where the customer could put their name, birthday, and address to join the birthday postcard mailing list.

I was the guy on the other end of that action. Picture Scrooge McDuck, but instead of swimming in gold coins, it's mountains of plastic orange baskets overflowing with rubber banded cards, and in-stead of Scrooge McDuck, it's me, and instead of swimming, it's more like hunching over at my desk trying to interpret the scrawl of some customer from Merrillville, Indiana, who several weeks previously had scribbled their information onto the back of this card while trying to scramble away from the pressure of the line of customers building up behind them.

I spent a lot of time inside that customer database in that first year, which surely created a comfort level with rows upon rows of data that needed to be sorted. When I went full time, I took over the weekly sales reporting for the company as well as using Excel to rec-oncile the thousands of dollars-worth of gift card sales and redemp-tions between the stores.

As the years went by there were many more opportunities for me to stretch my knowledge of Excel just a little further to solve problems for the company. I saw a real opportunity to improve the efficiency of the weekly chore of our store managers building their staff schedule. Since 1995, managers completed that task on paper, blocking out staff members' availability by shading out days off with a pencil and tracking their total hours with a calculator. Having once been responsible for that task at Store 3, I knew how cumbersome the whole process was. So, I wrote a whizbang spreadsheet that did all of that for them, using Google and a knowledgeable coworker as resources when I couldn't quite figure out how to do what I wanted to do.

Note the gradual and unintentional accumulation of knowledge across these years. There was never a single moment where I declared to the world: "Today is the day that I shall become awesome at Excel!" I just very slowly became rather awesome at Excel.

That made it easy for me to take what I'd slowly learned and achieved for granted. I'd hear "you should teach a class in Excel" from someone and I'd accept it as a compliment but never give it any serious thought. Until the umpteenth time I heard it. That time it broke through and that's just what I ended up doing – I created a basic class and an advanced class that I'd teach periodically to other Home Office employees. It made a difference for people! I continued to lead the class for years. And I never thought of myself as any kind of an Excel expert (and honestly, still do not). But I did end up accepting that what I do know about Excel is valuable and worth sharing.

How much of the knowledge and perspective you've gained across your life do you take for granted?

This is really important for two reasons: 1) You are decidedly more awesome than you think you are, and 2) what you've gained and take for granted could make a big difference for the people around you IF you would just own it and start to freely offer up what you've learned.

The Person in the Mirror is Your Friend—Act Accordingly

Another lightning bolt moment I experienced: I was in the middle of getting up and around some random weekday morning, brushing my teeth. Thinking some unkind thoughts about the guy who was brushing his teeth in the mirror and the size of his stomach. Not much of a morning pep talk, huh?

I found myself thinking about something a friend had said the day before, taking a swipe at himself for going bald. I called him out on it and told him that he'd better be nice to himself, or I'd have to kick his ass. Here I was the next morning doing the exact same thing to myself. Hi Pot, I'm Kettle, nice to meet you.

As I reflected on it further (and my teeth were getting really clean by this point), I realized that his baldness didn't matter to me at all. This feature he was insecure about was just something that I took at face value. It was just one of the many features that comprise who he is to me. I simply love the guy, and that's it.

That got me wondering—Could other people be viewing me in the same way I viewed him? Not at all with the same level of judgment that I cast upon myself? Not: "Ope, there's JD. Woof, he's fat." Just, "There's JD." Or perhaps more charitably: "There's JD, he's great!" Or even better: "There's JD, I love that guy!" And if it's possible (or perhaps even likely) that people see me that way, why not address myself from that perspective instead?

That epiphany is a great example of coming up with an empowering story. First of all, it's very likely that you are much, much, much more critical of yourself than other people who are in your orbit. So, when you are getting down on yourself, recognize that you are reacting to not-reality. You are responding to how you see yourself. And you, my friend, being a human and all, are extremely likely to have placed your "You Are Here" star in the completely wrong spot on the map of life.

So, if you can accept that you are not at all an objective judge of either who you are or how you are regarded by the people around you, perhaps you should approach those topics with a bit less certainty when you look at yourself in the mirror shortly after getting out of bed. Perhaps you should instead regard that reflection with a healthy dose of love and affirmation: "Hey, you! Good job getting up out of bed just now! <high-fiving your reflection> People love you! Isn't that cool? I think they're right! We're great! Let's go do this!!!" <bellows a challenge to the gods, begins brushing teeth, etc.>

Our Self-Perception Isn't Rooted in Objective Reality

This probably isn't a news flash for you, but it still bears a little talking through because chances are good that you need to hear this message. I expect we all know people, much like my literally-a-male-model friend who was self-conscious, who are clearly, fully, painfully, objectively beautiful or smart or fun or talented, who harbor beliefs that they're none of those things. And they're all a little bit exasperating, aren't they?

Well, guess what, so am I and so are you!

We're all untethered from objective reality when it comes to the subject of me, myself, and I.

It's not just that we can be mean with our self-talk. It's that our starting point on self-talk has no actual relationship to the reality of the situation.

I confronted that reality gap a few years ago. I didn't feel good about the way I looked. I characterized it as "I'm all belly." So over the course of a year or so, with a lot of work, I lost 60 pounds.

I felt accomplished when I looked at the scale. I liked that I was able to fit into a smaller shirt size. But when I looked in the mirror, I still felt sad about my appearance in the exact same way I did when I was 60 pounds heavier. What a rip off. All that sweat—and believe me, I mean a lot of sweat—and my brain was still short-changing me by coming up with the exact same emotional reaction when I looked in the mirror.

Because we're not tied to any objective reality when it comes to the subject of us, it's best not to trust our reactions, but instead to trust our outcomes...so for me and my weight loss, things like appreciating being able to fit into a smaller size shirt, or how I felt more comfortable on airplanes sitting next to strangers because I literally fit better into the seat, or how I was able to run faster when I went for a jog than I had been capable of when I was carrying more weight.

Our subconscious and our feelings can play tricks on us, warping our self-perception.

Stay focused on outcomes and you'll be standing on much firmer ground.

Get in Motion: Self-Perception and Seeing Yourself Clearly

Chances are good, given that you're reading this book, that you are human. And given that you're human, there is an excellent possibility that you have a slightly-warped to totally-bent perspective on what you're capable of and how others see you.

Let's dig into that, yeah? Time to grab a friend!

1) Write out a list of the things that you appreciate about the other person.

Their character traits, how they interact with the people around them, their skills, habits, and accomplishments, and their physical traits.

Speak your truth and be as detailed as possible in your observations. List out everything you can think of, even the very little things (for a sense of scale, that could even be the way they say a certain word, or a certain look they'll give you when you're together that you just love).

2) Write a list of things you appreciate about yourself.

Use the same process, but this time, you're the one who's in focus. Once you have completed your lists, it's time to get vulnerable.

3) Take turns reading what you wrote about the other person.

Read your list about them aloud, point by point. Your friend will note where you've written things about them that they also identified. Circle all of the items that you wrote that your friend didn't identify for themselves. Reverse roles and repeat.

4) Look over what your friend wrote for you, focusing on the things you missed for yourself.

Open up your heart as you read each one, recognizing that what your friend said is capital-T True about you, even if you don't see it for yourself.

5) Give your friend a huge hug and thank them for sharing with you.

Here's what's great about this activity – you get good brain chemicals flowing by starting the exercise by focusing all your good juju on your friend and vice versa. Chances are great that you'll each be able to point to things you do that you take for granted but still can have a big impact on others.

A friend did this for me when he pointed out that he can rely on me to bring a sense of silliness and levity into proceedings, especially when it's most needed. I hadn't noticed that I have that tendency, but he was right—I almost reflexively find a way to lighten the mood when things get unnecessarily heavy. By pointing this out, he has given me the opportunity to be more conscious about how I use that reflex, allowing me to turn it off or on as needed.

Chapter Ten

Stop Hitting Yourself!

Picture the scene, retold in countless movies, TV shows, and after school specials: the bully terrorizing the much smaller kid seated in front of him on the school bus. The bully is pulling out all of his favorite torture moves. Name calling. Kicking the seat back. Flicking the kid's earlobe. The bus driver is shockingly oblivious. The bully, emboldened, takes it further. A punch to the arm leads to a headlock and noogie combo, leading to the coup de grace moment of the bully grabbing his victim's wrists and making the poor schmo hit himself, all while saying, "Stop hitting yourself. Why are you hitting yourself?"

The bully is the villain of that scene. Maybe of the whole movie. Not especially likable and not someone who you would likely pick as a role model, right? And yet, chances are better than good that you impersonate that bully on the regular. Your favorite victim? The person looking back at you in that mirror.

When you look in the mirror, what do you think? What words come to mind? Is your brain the bullying type? If so, let's look at how you can arm yourself with a little mental jujitsu so you can slip out of your inner bully's grasp.

Me, Myself, and My Inner Bully

As I mentioned in chapter 9, there are times when my inner bully shows up, especially when I look at myself in the mirror first thing in the morning.

On those kinds of mornings, I'll sigh and think to myself things like, "Ugh, gross." Or perhaps "So. Much. Belly." Or if it's an especially dark morning, "How can Megan be attracted to you?"

Nasty piece of work, my inner bully! I would never, ever say that to someone else, but that inner bully can show up without an invitation and start making me hit myself, day after day, with that kind of negative self-talk.

Like I mentioned, the self-talk doesn't vary based on how much I weigh; even when we're talking about a 60-pound difference. Sixty pounds is the stuff that before and after pictures are made of. And yet my bully shows up with the exact same script in his hand, ready to act it all out the exact same way.

But, I have noticed that the way he shows up correlates strongly to whether I'm making good choices in my life. If I'm feeling positive about my decisions, for example how much I had to eat or drink the night before or how much I worked out, it's like my inner bully takes on a begrudging appreciation. "Huh. Okay, you're trying. Long way to go, but you're trying." "Not bad, not bad. Not great. But not bad." "I can see some progress. Things are looking better from where you were."

But if I went on a junk food binge the night before or had a couple too many beers, he shows up sounding like the drill sergeant from the movie Full Metal Jacket telling his son he's disappointed in him. "Get your bleeping bleep act together, DeRuiter, you slob! You bleeping disaster! You call that trying? I can't even bleeping look at you I'm so bleeping disappointed."

You might think your negative self-talk is harmless. The same thing as lightly teasing a friend. Here's why that's just not true. First of all, I'd push in all my chips on the idea that the sort of things that you say out loud are a lot more tame than the unsaid things you aim at yourself. Negative self-talk will always be much nastier than the things that come out of your mouth, aimed at people you love.

The other problem here is the way you talk to yourself has a direct impact on how you behave. How you behave and the things that you choose to do (and not do) in your daily life IS your life.

If your negative self-talk represents a steady stream of self-limiting beliefs, it's more than just teasing. You're hurting your own potential in life!

Imagine how having a steady stream of thinking like "I'll never be thin," "I'll never be as good as your sister," or "I am dumb" could insinuate themselves into your life! If you think "I'll never be thin," then why would you bother getting serious about exercise or learning to prepare lower-calorie, delicious and fulfilling meals? Or if "I am dumb" is a drumbeat in your life, why would you bother to go out for continuing education opportunities in your workplace or take a risk to take on a project that would require you to stretch yourself beyond what you already comfortably know?

If you have some recurring negative themes in your self-talk, you're going to want to start working on a replacement. This dynamic is very similar to what I talked about in chapter 4. You can rewrite your self-talk script and build up a reflex in your mind to respond quickly and confidently when your inner bully saunters into the room.

For example, when I have those low moments in the morning, looking in the bathroom mirror, I answer, "Ugh. Gross" and "So. Much.

Belly" with "I am loved" and "I am powerful." It reminds me that my self-worth exists outside of my appearance and that I am empowered to choose change.

Just as it did for me on my morning commute, with practice, this reflex moves faster and faster through my brain. It's not about trying to prevent the inner bully from showing up - all kinds of thoughts are going to go whizzing through our brains across the course of the day--6,200 on average, according to a 2020 study. We can't stop them from occurring. It's what we choose to do with them that gives us our freedom back.

If my response to "Ugh. Gross," was to sigh and think, "You're right. I am gross. I am a disgusting slob" it would be like inviting the bully to come in and make himself at home. And there he would reside, in the front of my mind, chipping away at my self-worth, day after day.

Instead, I know how to quiet him. Building up this reflexive thinking allows me to get back to productive and healthy thought patterns (including, by the way, investing in my physical health) and also provides my brain with fuel that powers my self-worth. Some inner bullies might be too powerful to be talked down like this—if you're trapped in a negative self-talk loop get some extra help from a professional, that's what they're there for!

Meanwhile, you might have noticed that "I am loved" and "I am powerful" sound a lot like affirmations. They are! The distinction is that these can be used as a reaction to negative thoughts rather than something that's part of a morning routine, for instance. Hey, let's actually talk a bit more about affirmations!

Cozy Up to the Squirm

If you are of a certain age, the idea of affirmations was a subject of *Saturday Night Live* ridicule: "I'm good enough. I'm smart enough. And doggonit, people like me." Stuart Smalley, a character performed by Al Franken, said into his mirror.

I think it was specifically because of this skit that when the subject of affirmations got raised, I would back away slowly like Homer Simpson fading into the shrubbery. I believe that SNL did to affirmations what Jaws did to sharks. So squirmy a presentation that some of us don't even want to dip a toe in.

It was my involvement with our LifeLab workshops that led me to look affirmations square in the eye. One of the workshops has a homework assignment to try out affirmations, saying these big, nice, affirming things to yourself while looking yourself in the mirror. It got me to dip a toe in, but I didn't manage to build a habit out of it. I think that was in part because my moments in front of the mirror, especially during working weekdays, are hurried. The other part, I suppose, was that residual Stuart Smalley awkwardness.

It wasn't until just in the last few months that I've built up a solid affirmations routine. It's part of my feel-good freight train: a few minutes of meditation followed by expressing gratitude for three moments from the day before, followed by visualizing five little scenes from my future once I achieve my dreams (I describe this in chapter 12), followed by five affirmations.

I started with three affirmations and have increased it to five. Here's my methodology:

Affirmation #1: Parts of my character that I'm proud of and confident in

Affirmation #2: Characteristics I have but am developing

Affirmation #3: Focused on a challenge I want to overcome

Affirmation #4: Something that builds up my self-confidence

Affirmation #5: Something pointed directly at a personal goal

You ready to feel the squirm? I mean, maybe you won't feel all wiggly and weird about this, but I am UNCOMFORTABLE. I'm going to share what my actual affirmations are to provide an example of what these come out looking like for me, at the time of writing.

"I am smart, funny, and hard-working." I have gotten a lifetime of feedback from the people in my life about these traits. I feel super uncomfortable claiming them here in front of you, but despite that, I know that these are the characteristics that I've leaned into the most over the course of my life, and I know that other people value in my interactions with them.

"I am loving, supportive, and a challenger." These are characteristics that others have pointed out. In fact, these were specifically inspired by feedback I received from a group of people I coach at the BIGGBY Home Office. I still have some internal "yeah, buts" about the nice things they've had to say. I love and accept their compliments and can see the truth of them in me and in the way that I engage the people in my life, but I know that I'm either A) not consistent enough in expressing them, or B) I have some inner monologue that can at times run counter to these characteristics. I'm 75 percent of the way to where I want to be.

"I am courageous and capable." There have been moments across this year where I have felt the tug to take some big leaps in my life. I've hesitated. This affirmation is to help me nurture in myself the idea that I have in the past—and will in the future—stepped way outside of my comfort zone and beyond that, taking those leaps are worthwhile because I am more capable in reality than I sometimes feel on the inside. Why hello there, imposter syndrome, nice of you to show up.

"People admire me for me." This is something that I have frequently been surprised about across the course of my life, because I take myself for granted. This has come up repeatedly for me within the world of BIGGBY where I'm go-

> ing through an experience, basically stumbling my way forward, unsure of exactly what the right thing to do is, just busy being myself and later on I find out that someone thought that I was exceptional in the way I handled the thing. There are other versions of this, but the baseline concept that I locked into this affirmation is that somehow, some way, me just being me in a way that I totally take for granted is something that the people in my life appreciate and rely on me for. Weird! But cool!
>
> **"I can be 200 pounds if I choose to change the way I eat and drink."** This is the other new addition to my routine. I'm making this small investment in myself each morning, centering these words in the front of my brain, in a deliberate attempt to better equip myself to interrupt well-worn habits that have contributed to me carrying more weight around on my body than is healthy or productive. It's a simple reminder that I have agency in how I live my life, calorically.

Okay, yep, I am sweating just thinking about people in my life reading that section. And not just because I'm overweight! Ha!

Self-Deprecating Humor

See what I did there? How's that for an understated segue?

We all have that friend who makes it a habit to talk badly about themselves in a joking sort of way. "Just the Queen of Awkward over here, no big deal." "Well, yes, that would have been a good idea, but instead, I did this <gestures to disaster> because I am me." "What's round, uncomfortable, and has two thumbs? This guy..."

Or perhaps that has become a friend group's entire way of being with each other. Texting groups that are an endless stream of gifs of dumpster fires, cats manically typing on keyboards, or people tripping and falling all being captioned with things like "My year so far," "My brain today," "Me trying to be an adult," etc.

Self-deprecating humor can be useful, but it can also be harmful. Like me holding a chef's knife above a cutting board full of vegetables versus my dog pulling the knife out of the dishwasher and running around the house with it.

I think that joking around like that, if done only occasionally, is just fine! Self-deprecating humor (okay, typing that phrase out again and again is starting to make me feel sleepy, so we're going to call it SDH from here on out) can do a few helpful things in social situations and inside of a relationship.

It can be disarming! I can think of plenty of times in my life where it's helped me to settle into a room with a group of strangers. Across the first 10 years of my time with the BIGGBY Home Office, I led hundreds of training sessions, providing me with the chance to see this play out about a zillion times.

Picture it: Day one of barista training the week before the store opens for business. The group assembles, it's eight in the morning. I have maybe 10 new hires in front of me, with an average age of 21, which includes the empty nester. They're a mix of sleepy, excited, and nervous. Starting a new job is tough enough, but who's this guy from corporate?

I start class by welcoming them and introducing myself, telling the short version of my story of how I came to be there, which includes the bit about me failing my way forward from a science degree in college to an English degree. It's a small tidbit to which I'd add others throughout the week. The cumulative effect is that it humanizes me and helps to quiet down the very human part of my trainees' brains that makes them uptight around someone who is an authority figure.

Now imagine if, on the other hand, that in my three-minute intro, that it was littered with SDH. Making cracks about how many pounds of Caramel Marvel (the flagship flavored lattes of BIGGBY) I'm carrying around my waist, about how much terrible credit card debt that I had wracked up, how lonely it was to be a single guy in my early twenties with no real prospects because I worked all the time and wouldn't want to date someone inside the company, about how crummy my apartment was and how sketchy my neighbors, about how it had been years since I'd bothered to go to a dentist or see a doctor, and on and on.

Can you just picture the uncomfortable glances they'd be shooting each other out of the corner of their eyes and the nervous laughs?

A little bit of SDH can settle the room, taking the fancy-pants corporate guy down to an approachable level. A lotta' bit of SDH would have been a signal that I had issues with self-love, self-confidence, self-forgiveness, body image, or other eating-me-away-from-the-inside issues.

Here's some good news about SDH: Because, by its very nature, it's an out-loud expression, it makes it rather easy to solicit support from the people in your life. Ditto, btw, if your Inner Bully is an Inner and Out-Loud Bully, leading to you calling yourself names or swearing at yourself out in the open where friends and family can observe your behavior.

If you have the tendency to verbally run yourself down, whether it's bullying comments or jokes, your friends can start to supply those replacements for you. In fact, they may already be doing that since that's the natural tendency. "Shhhh, stop saying that, you are beautiful." "Honey, please, you are brilliant and talented, so stop saying that."

You'll also need to take a hard look at yourself and make an inventory about what you have going on internally when you're making those comments and jokes. Are you seeking attention and looking for people to affirm you? Are you trying to discharge some awkward feelings? Or are you doing it reflexively—an unconscious expression of your feelings about yourself?

If you take that inventory and find that it might be part of a negative or self-serving thought pattern, and especially if it's mostly unconscious, you'll want to get your friends to start calling it out. They don't even need to provide the replacement comment--it would be good practice for you to correct it yourself with phrases such as: "I am loved," "I am powerful," "I will figure out this bleeping printer.".

Accepting Compliments

If you were raised inside of a certain sensibility, whether that was formed by your parents, friends, teachers, or the culture of your community, when someone serves you with a compliment, you react in bullet-time, dodging in a flurry of arms, bending over backward, the kind comments whizzing by without having a chance to touch you. "Not at all; I was just lucky!" "Oh, this old thing?" "Pshaw! You're nuts!"

Or it might look more like another scene from *The Matrix*. The compliment comes flying in at you, and with all of your humble kung fu jujitsu karate warrior-ness, you grab it and redirect it, so it flies on by you at a new target. "It was just a solid team effort." "You should see my sister, she's the smart one in the family." "I could have done so much better than that if I had more time to prepare."

Any of that sound familiar? Are you impervious to compliments? Doesn't matter how earnest or specific the person is when complimenting you, it slides right off, like rain on a turtle's back?

What's going on with that, do you suppose? Where does that conditioning come from? I say "conditioning" because I expect you've been doing it your whole life. You probably learned it as you learned to speak–hearing it all around you. It's not at all your fault.

"Fault?" you might ask. "What do you mean my fault? You act

like I'm perpetuating emotional abuse or something like that!"

Ah, well, you took it a little further than I intended it, in that case. But you do have my gist! By batting away compliments, you are both denying yourself the opportunity to build up your reserves of self-love as well as missing a chance to build some extra relationship with the person who is offering you the compliment.

That anti-compliment reflex is a lot like feeling squirmy about the idea of saying kind things to yourself in the form of affirmations. As if you don't believe that you're worthy of the nice thoughts.

You. Are. Worthy!

Time to start building up a new reflex. The simplest thing to do is to say, "Thank you!" and then rock that blush if it spreads across your cheeks. You might find that you need to tighten up the speed of your reflexes. You might first find that you're halfway into your Aw Shucks Pose before realizing it. Correct yourself if you have to! "It was just beginner's lu....er, what I mean to say is, 'Thank you.'"

And if you feel like you're somehow undeserving of it, consider doing two things. First, hyperextend your thank you – "Oh geez, that's really too kind, thank you!" It still allows you to receive the compliment but demonstrates that it hit you unexpectedly, which might be enough to scratch that self-conscious itch that's part of your normal reflexes.

Second, take note of that compliment. Like, literally. Write it down. Then come back to it later and do a little thinking – What is it about that compliment that felt difficult to receive? Was it something inside of you that reacted to the words themselves? Was it something about the context...either something about the person giving you the compliment or the other people within earshot that made it seem more appropriate to try to dodge it? Might there be some additional work you can do for yourself based on this reaction?

Oh and don't think that I've forgotten to circle back to the bit about how the other person fits into this whole equation. When you are able to graciously and fully receive a compliment, you get to reciprocate a little bit of the emotion that person is extending to you, providing another small bit of relationship-building between the two of you.

Now is it possible that the person is extending the compliment in some sort of disingenuous way? Sure. Yep. There are people who will offer praise because they think it's the right thing to do based on social cues or some outcome they're trying to achieve (for example, complimenting a boss because they're trying to curry favor with them...I'm picturing scenes from *The Sopranos* where Tony Soprano's crew is laughing in a forced way to lame jokes).

So, there's a small chance that someone is being manipulative with their praise, but I hope you keep that in proportion and think about it in terms of 1 person in 100, not 1 in 10. If it feels like 1 in 10 to you, you need new friends and/or coworkers or you need to reevaluate your perspective (for example...are you offering false praise 1 in 10 times, or 1 in 100...if being disingenuous or manipulative is part of your way of being it would make sense that you would see that same thing reflected back all around you).

For me, while it's possible that I might get a little squirmy, I think that, more often than not, I'm able to receive the compliment with gratitude. I try to extend praise wherever I see fit, and I think that at this point in my life, false praise is like .0001 percent of it. I love being able to compliment people on the things I see in them that strike me as special in some way, earned with good effort, or otherwise charming and surprising.

In fact, to say it differently, I fairly well thrive on praise. It's one of my top two love languages/languages of appreciation in the workplace. I have always tried to go the extra mile and I always appreciate it when those efforts and the results get noted with praise. I try to pass that along in my life as often as I can.

What is your way of being around praise and compliments? How giving are you, and how closely does that mirror how well you receive compliments? If you're not where you wish you could be on this trait, it's something that you can go to work on, and for that matter, more easily than many of the other areas I've outlined in this book. Wanna get going?

Get in Motion: You and Your Self-Talk and Self-Love

Alright, it's time to get squirmy. Time for some actual IRL looking-at-yourself-in-the-mirror-ing.

Go stand in front of a mirror and give yourself a good once-over. Let's see what comes up.

1. What words come to mind, without trying, when you look at yourself in the mirror?
2. Now, try a little harder: Describe yourself, to yourself, out loud. Focus on physical details first, then move on to describing your own character to your reflection.
3. How squirmy did you get? Why, do you think?
4. Considering the way you thought of yourself and then how you described yourself, what stands out as negative descriptions?
5. Does anything stand out as flat-out mean? Like the kind of thing you would never even consider saying to a friend or loved one?
6. List out each negative or mean thing that you thought or said about yourself in a column on a sheet of paper. Next, write out a list of replacement words and phrases that would

reverse those negative thoughts.

7. Look at the replacement words and phrases that you wrote – they are the stuff of affirmations. If you regularly struggle with that kind of thinking, in the same way that I do, I command you, as if I were wearing a fancy crown engraved with the words King of Making You Feel Better About Yourself, to take the one that makes you feel most squirmy and the one that makes you feel least squirmy and in fact maybe even a little bit nice, and turn them into affirmations.
8. Set yourself a calendar appointment or an alarm so you don't forget. I want you to say those nice words to yourself, out loud, for the next seven days. You can pick the time and the place, but you're not allowed to miss.
9. After your first time, and after your seventh time, I want you to answer the question: Now, how do you feel?
10. Because a 10-item list just feels better to me. That's all.

Section Three

Can You See Where You're Going?

Knowing what you want to be (and do) with your life and knowing how you want to be as a person are crucial to the process of waking up and getting free of the momentum of life.

You need to be able to see a path in order to choose to take it. If you're stumbling through life blind to how many options you have, you're sure to miss opportunities again and again.

Without a sense of direction or purpose, you're left to being carried along day to week to month to year.

Doesn't mean you can't be happy, but I assure you, you will be missing out on so much more that life has to offer you.

I spent the majority of my life not knowing the answers to what and how I wanted to be. I didn't have specific dreams. As a young man, I knew I wanted a girlfriend—that wasn't so much a dream as it was an urgent need! I wanted to do well in school, though I think that was more my parent's doing. They had high expectations, so that was just part of my script. I knew I needed a job so I could make money so I could buy things. "Things" meant being able to buy DVDs of all my favorite movies and books by the bagful. College, get married, career, kids...all part of the plan, but really just part of the script.

I also didn't give a second's thought to the idea that I even could be a different type of person. I certainly knew I could learn things—facts and skills—and even enjoy it. But just kinda' figured that I am who I am. I'm so glad that my work with BIGGBY proved that wrong, and I'm a little sad it took as long as it did for me to have that particular breakthrough.

Do you dream about the kind of life you want to live? Did you know that your brain is a magic machine, just waiting to help you turn those dreams into reality?

Sure sure, your brain is out to sabotage you sixteen different ways, as we've covered, but it's also an incredible tool that you can use to intentionally build a life you love.

Chapter 11

Let's Dream a Little Dream, Shall We?

Visioning is the act of intentional dreaming. Of choosing to sit down and dream about what your future will hold and committing that vision to paper (or an app if you prefer). If you let the thoughts pass by like a daydream, that is all they will be...passing whims, quickly vanished.

The act of recording the dream on paper makes the dream more real. It becomes tactile. Something that can be returned to again and again. Because you've made a record of them, because you'll return to them again and again, they will begin to come true.

Sounds magical, no? It works. It's spooky how well it works.

There are two schools of thought on how it works. You actually don't need to know how it works for it to work for you, by the way. But if I were you, reading these assertions, I would most definitely want to understand what was going on before I bothered with any of it.

The first school of thought is that visioning is an act of inviting a higher power and/or the universe itself to present you with the things that you desire. By speaking it out loud, by writing it down, by investing your attention and energy into it, you will manifest it all into your life.

This reminds me of a Bible verse that stuck with me throughout my life, Matthew 7:7: "Ask and it will be given to you; seek and you will find; knock and the door will be opened to you." The verse comes from the Sermon on the Mount, where Jesus is laying out all kinds of good advice, including, five verses later, the Golden Rule.

The second school of thought, which I personally ascribe to, is that visioning works because of a healthy dose of brain science. When you dream with intent, committing your dreams by writing them down, you get to take advantage of frequency bias, or if you're fancy, the Baader-Meinhof phenomenon.

You may not be familiar with either term, but I'm certain you've experienced it in your life. Have you had the experience of buying a car and then suddenly seeing that same car everywhere on the road? That's the Baader-Meinhof phenomenon.

Meanwhile, on the other side of that coin, what's happening there? Think about it. Those cars were out there on the road, all around you, zooming by just as frequently. You "saw" them but didn't actually register them in the same way—they lacked any further or special meaning (so long as they stayed in their lane).

Pause for a second to think about the broader implication here - what else are you missing? Our brains are amazingly strong filters for information and sensations. We'll get into the brain science of it in chapter 12, but for now, just consider that if you're able to not see certain cars until something helps them break through your filter, the exact same thing is happening with missed opportunities.

And that's why when you write down your dreams, you're very likely to see them come true. Writing down those words creates a little bit of space in that filter in your brain. As you stumble forward through your day-to-day, you'll become much more likely to actually see the opportunities that will bring you one step closer to your dreams.

Again: It does not matter if you remember or believe either explanation that I've presented here. I promise that if you make a habit of writing down your dreams, they will start to come true!

How I Visioned My Way into a Demotion

I've been inside the practice of visioning for seven years as I write this. This was another gift from the process of us launching Leadership Forums. Many of these groups would read books together, one of which was *The E-Myth Revisited*, by Michael Gerber. It's a great read for anyone who owns or wants to start their own business, and my favorite chapter is titled Primary Aim.

Gerber helps readers to focus on the idea that the business—owning it, making it profitable—is not the end. It's a means. So why be in business for yourself? What are you doing it for? What do you want your life to be like day-to-day? He includes 12 questions to help you start thinking about this.

This is how I answered the question about what I want my life to look like, that first time:

> *To remain happy in my work--challenged and fulfilled. To laugh, at home, every day, to have a visible positive effect on the people around me, to maintain my health into later life, to*

retire when Megan does, to a cottage on Lake Michigan, and leave a lasting impact.

Writing down those words had a nearly immediate effect on the choices I was making, particularly because of the line "to maintain my health into later life." When I sat down to consider what I wanted my life to look like, I realized that:

1. I wanted to remain active (including physically) into my later life
2. The choices I was making at the time were way out of line with that desire

For example, I hadn't been to see a doctor or a dentist in close to 15 years. That kind of combination of apathy and avoidance is not a solid recipe for maintaining my health into later life. That, in combination with my eating and exercise habits, was more of a recipe for being a denture-wearing diabetic by the time I hit 50!

So, I decided it was time to buck up the amount of courage required to risk a potential tut-tutting from them both and schedule appointments. Did I have a bunch of cavities and early-onset diabetes? No, I did not. I had two cavities and high blood pressure. Felt like an even exchange for all those years of neglect.

That is the value of actually writing down your vision for life. It's no longer a bunch of free-floating wishes and hopes, but a concrete statement that you can measure your life against. Because you've written it down, and especially if you review what you've written regularly, it creeps into the nooks and crannies of your daily experiences. You can see the ways that you're not living up to your dream, and it helps you see the opportunity for change when you stumble across it.

There is also an incredible amount of value in sharing your vision with others, if you can muster the courage. I remember feeling butterflies in my stomach the first time I shared what I'd written down with my wife. "What does it mean if she doesn't like what I wrote? If she doesn't want the same things for us?" Ditto sharing my vision for how I want my career to develop with my peers.

Going into my second time doing the Primary Aim exercise, I wrote these words, answering the question of how I wanted to be spending my time two years later:

> *I will be free of day-to-day management of the Brand Sphere, focused instead on... [helping] people create the best versions of themselves, as well as to be out in the world, creating connections that help me learn, as well as provide opportunities to further my personal and professional goals. I will begin giving presentations outside of the Annual Franchise Meeting, including on behalf of the Boost Sphere, and in the community. I will do all of this while enjoying my 40–45 hour work weeks each week.*

Looking back at my answer, there's a lot packed in there.

Let's start with "I will be free of day-to-day management of the Brand Sphere..." It's so clear, in those four starting words, that I was unhappy in my daily work life in that time period. It's not that there wasn't a lot of good stuff, too, but it had little to do with the main duties of my role. I wanted out but I didn't know it yet, not in the front of my mind.

All of it came true, most of it happening within that two-year time frame. Not the way I pictured, though. I came close to being fired. Pulled into a room and given options, most of which involved leaving the company that I loved. But that's not what happened.

Instead I took a demotion and they moved me to the BOOST Sphere. I was decidedly "free" of the day-to-day management of the Brand Sphere. It was a stressful time, especially the part where Megan and I had to reckon with the consequences of the corresponding pay cut.

But my day-to-day work life improved dramatically. I suddenly became responsible for work that I loved doing. Alongside my teammates Brie and Laura, I became a coach to my coworkers and developed and led personal-growth-focused workshops. It was all directly in line with my desire to "help people create the best versions of themselves."

Meanwhile, I took over *The Moonshot Guidebook*, reimagined it, and expanded it, eventually leading to the book being published by Conscious Capitalism Press. This led to me creating connections and giving presentations outside of the world of BIGGBY. All while "enjoying 40–45 hour work weeks" instead of the 50–60 hours I was averaging in my previous role.

Pretty dramatic, no? That's one example of many that I could highlight from my experiences with visioning. I've become a gardener and a really solid home cook. I've run a half marathon and hiked cross country for a full marathon's-worth of miles. I'm a board game designer. I've continued to laugh at home every day. I'm writing this book! All of these accomplishments started as dreams I captured on paper!

You might be saying, "Yeah, but look at all of these accomplishments I have achieved, and I don't bother with visioning!" To which I reply, "That's amazing! I'm happy for you! But what might you be leaving on the table?"

Visioning isn't the only path to achievement, but it's a surefire way of helping you align your short-term accomplishments with long-term aspirations. It will take your high-achiever-ness and help you channel all that positive activity in a way that leads you to more powerful results.

The Power of Sharing

I asserted that there's a lot of value in sharing your vision, but kinda' breezed right past the how and why of it. Sharing your vision is valuable because it makes it more likely that your vision will come true, regardless of whether you buy into either of the woo woo or brain science schools of thought.

Step one is writing your dreams down. Step two is sharing them with the people in your life.

We've already established that writing down your vision is a key part of making your dreams come true, as opposed to leaving them as daydreams floating down the river of your mind. The dreams become more real on paper (or in an app, or on a vision board, or on an app for vision boards...more on vision boards at the end of this chapter). The first thing that sharing does for you is it takes that bit of realness gained from writing it down and it quadruples it.

When you read your words out loud, not just to an empty room, your cat, or an attentive audience of stuffed animals, but to another human—ideally one who you care about and who cares about you—your brain is going to start processing the words differently. I can't predict exactly how it will turn out for you, dear reader, but for me, it looks a bit like this, almost like a computer program running with a bunch of background processes:

> Program: <Jeremy starts reading his *Moonshot Guidebook* answers to a group of people>
>
> Background Process 1: Jeremy thinks, "Oh, that's interesting. Huh. Is that still true? I wrote that four months ago. Huh."
>
> Background Process 2: Jeremy thinks while processing the words he's just about to read, "Ooh, that's feeling a little

extra vulnerable to share that tidbit. Maybe we skip? Er, maybe share it? But with some extra story to help make it not sound so...that?"

Background Process 3: Jeremy evaluates what he just finished saying as he continues to read, "Is that something I can achieve? Is that too big? Too small? Too much or little?

In short, I started running the words that I wrote through a whole new set of filters and seeing it with a very different lens than when it was just me and the empty page. Sometimes, it means I'll make a change right there in the middle of sharing, crossing out or adding words, adding detail, or striking something that no longer feels like it's true to who I am today.

It doesn't stop there for me, though. There's something else that happens for me when I share, something way in the background. The processes illustrated above are the sort of questions that pop into the front of my mind as I'm reading my words. I'm completely in-the-moment conscious of what I'm thinking. But somewhere deep inside me, perhaps in a spiritual cubicle, and looking down his nose at the goblin doing his thing with the lever, is my Accountability Gnome.

He is very concerned with keeping track of the promises I'm making to people around me. He's got a spreadsheet with lots of columns and tabs, color-coded and running some macros. He's watching through thick glasses perched atop a pointy nose that refract light onto his rosy cheeks and when I share what I want for my life—what I intend to do—clickity clackity (he has a very loud mechanical keyboard, I've decided) and now just like that, he's got those statements filed away, noted, linked, cross-tabbed and ready to pull up at a moment's notice sometime in the future.

Oddly, he often seems to be on a coffee break when I'm making promises to myself, but when I'm talking to someone else, he's there, looking over the rim of his glasses at me, adding what I've said to my commitment ledger.

When I share my dreams with the people in my life, I feel more accountable to those words. It's not that I think I'm promising that I will do all these exact things. When I make a promise to a person it's a solemn oath in my book and I'll do the thing to the letter and I'm fully conscious when I'm making that level of commitment to another person. This isn't a promise, but still, when I'm sharing my dreams, somewhere deep in the background for me, the words are a bit more real than they used to be, and because of that, I need to take them just a little more seriously. People are watching. My Gnome friend is watching. The Goblin is off scratching himself or something. He doesn't really factor in.

Meanwhile, amidst all the cool stuff happening for me in my brain, there's also some cool stuff happening in my friends' brains, too. This goes back to the Baader-Meinhof effect. By sharing, I create a little space for me and my dreams in my friend's brain filters too. In fact, that was another cool part of the road that led from doing visioning work straight to *The Moonshot Guidebook* being published.

Those words I mentioned above about beginning to give presentations outside the world of BIGGBY found fertile ground in the mind of our workplace culture consultant (and in the years since, friend), Nathan Havey. He called me one day in late 2018 after I made my move into the BOOST Sphere, to see if I could take something off of his plate for him. As a very active member in the broader Conscious Capitalism community, and at that time, especially in the state of Michigan, he had been invited to speak at the annual meeting of the Conscious Capitalism Great Lakes Bay Area chapter. He had a conflict and called to see if I could fill in.

Literally the beginning of a dream come true for me. In May of 2019, at the meeting, I shared about the things we had done at the

BIGGBY Home Office to activate our higher purpose. The room was full of business professionals for many different area organizations. Among those present was Alexander McCobin, the then-CEO of Conscious Capitalism Inc., there to give the keynote. I was up next, and I think it's legitimately fair to say that I hit my mark that day, generating an enthusiastic response from the audience and a lot of great follow-up conversations.

Within a few months, Alexander would be signing off on our deal for Conscious Capitalism Press to publish *The Moonshot Guidebook*. In 2020, Laura and I presented about BIGGBY culture at the national (though sadly, COVID-forced virtual) annual Conscious Capitalism meeting. Not too long after that, Alexander took me up on my offer to facilitate a series of *Moonshot Guidebook* sharing activities with him and the rest of the CCI staff. This coming month I'll be kicking off a series of sessions with the 100 Months to Change group, a global coalition to affect real climate change measures. All because Nathan heard my words years ago and found an opportunity for me.

I hope the same thing happens inside the 100 MTC group—even a small impact there could create some really amazing things in the lives of these folks and in their work to, um, save humanity. Woof. I love it here.

So, yeah, I believe in the power of sharing your dreams with the people in your life.

Forecasting and the Fog

I've had the opportunity to coach hundreds of people as they've began the process of visioning. It's such a privilege to be able to work with people as they get started shaping their dreams and building a future world for themselves. It has also put me in the position to observe the pitfalls and hurdles that people—myself included—commonly fall into.

#1 Don't try to predict your future.

Visioning isn't about looking at where you are today and trying to make some bets about where you'll end up in 20 years. Yikes. Even typing that made me feel uptight. That idea sounds zero percent fun and entirely misses the point of visioning.

Instead of trying to forecast your future, write down what you want without the burden of worrying about how much it might cost in time or money or whether you think you might possibly ever have the opportunity. If you have a burning desire to be the first human to set foot on Mars, write it down! Heck, why not become a time traveler, too! Write down what you want to be, how you want to be as a person, where you want to go, what you want to do—all without giving a fig about how likely it is. You can worry about how to make it all happen later.

#2 Don't worry about foggy vision.

This builds off of #1. If, when you sit down to do some dreaming, you can't see very far at all into the future, don't panic and don't give up. Just write what you can see. I've seen this most frequently with people who know their interests tend to shift around quickly across time and don't want to pin themselves down. I've also seen a version of this with parents—especially moms—who have become so accustomed to subverting their own desires for the good of their family that they are uncomfortable thinking about, let alone writing down, what they want to spend their lives doing.

So, if you're having a hard time pulling the full picture into focus, that's okay!

If what you want changes later today, that's okay! You're not etching anything into granite here, it's easy to go back and change it.

The important thing is to get moving.

It's like walking along a pathway shrouded with dense fog. Standing still, you can only see a little way in front of you. But if you walk to that furthest point you can see, you'll be able to see that much further ahead from your new position. As you continue to repeat the process, you cover a lot of ground, and see a lot of new things, and eventually the fog itself will clear.

Write down whatever part of your vision you can see right now, today, from where you stand.

Building a visioning practice will do the same thing for you. Start today, write as much as you can see from where you stand. Go out, live some life, let several months pass, and return to it. Things might look different from where you are now, so write the new stuff you can see for yourself and leave behind what you wrote before that suddenly seems wrong. And repeat. And repeat. And repeat.

Across time, across years, you will begin to see your future more clearly. You will notice that patterns emerge. While some of the specific things that excited you once upon a time will change, it might be that there's a common theme that ran through them all. For example, I can see how my curiosity and love of learning informed multiple pastimes, whether that was learning how to play guitar or getting deeply into geocaching, board games, and now, cooking.

#3 Write your truth, not what others would want you to.

Whether we're talking friends, parents, teachers, bosses, or a significant other, I expect that you know what it's like to have someone's expectations placed around your neck and finding it a really uncomfortable fit. Perhaps you've made mistakes like I have, following someone else's inspiration for your life instead of following your own star.

Listen, it's a natural mistake to make, particularly if those expectations land on you at a time when you're not all that sure yourself what you want to do. Don't beat yourself up about it. But when it comes time for you to write down your dreams, please do make sure that they are yours alone. If you mix in things that you feel like you "should" write down, you're diluting the power of your own dreams. It would be like mixing water into a car's gas tank. You will end up sputtering when you could have been running smoothly toward achieving your dreams.

Dashboard of Dreams

I am not a crafter. I mean, I build things here and there, but not in an artsy-crafty sort of way. If it involves glue sticks, scissors, beads, crochet, or bedazzling, it's just not my thing. I tend to get impatient when working on what I think of as overly-fussy projects. I love taking on big projects to improve my yard, moving hundreds of pounds of earth, wielding the chainsaw, or building something with my hands, right up until it's time to get out the level and measuring tape to finesse things until they're just right. Then, I tend to get a little impatient. It feels like the ratio of the amount of progress versus the amount of effort goes way down.

So, the idea of building a vision board always struck me as not-a-me thing for a few reasons. First, there's the whole clipping pictures out of magazines (or whatever) step. It gives me uncomfy feelings, echoes from, perhaps, elementary or middle school art classes where I was just fumbling along, maybe being a little upset about being left-handed and struggling to use the standard righty-only scissors.

Beyond that, it just seemed...cheesy. And materialistic. Don't get me wrong, I like the idea of owning stuff. But seeing the idea of vision boards portrayed in movies seemed like it needed to involve fancy sports cars (meh), mansions (we'd never need that kind of space), and other swag that I really didn't care about.

That was just it—THOSE vision boards weren't for me. They were filled with ideas and things that weren't all that exciting to me, and so no surprise, I wasn't very excited to get started. That was a mistake. I wish I would have gotten started using this visioning tool back when I was in high school, because I found that once I took the time to build my vision board with the people, places, things, and pursuits that I cared about, it became suuuper fun. Now that I have a vision board, it feels like a dashboard for my future life – Here are the experiences I want to have. The feelings I want to cultivate. The things I'd like someday to own.

My first try at building my own vision board was an outcome of working with Alisha on building out a workshop series to help people sort out who they wanted to be. She had read and loved Jen Sincero's *You Are a Badass* and one of the chapters deals with building vision boards. We included it in the workshop curriculum, so once it was time for us to start leading sessions, I did the work right alongside the folks in the workshop.

I built my V.1 using the Pinterest app, which is rather well-suited to the task. It even accommodates my preference for organization, allowing me to create different sections for the different categories of pins. I created a section for cooking and filled it with photos of beautiful and tasty-looking cuisine. Another section was for travel, pinning roughly a zillion (okay just 121) pictures of places I would love to spend time across my life. The pins racked up quickly, and suddenly I had a lot of inspiring images that spoke to how I wanted to live and spend my time.

The disadvantage of solely relying on Pinterest as a vision board is that while finding inspiring photos is easy, you can't become inspired by them if you almost never go back to browse through them. There are vision board apps that help you avoid this pitfall by letting you create an image that can be used for your phone's wallpaper, helping it be more visible day-to-day, but the number of individual images you can see is very limited.

I recognized these as limitations as I experimented with them, so when I was thinking about ideas that I could pursue for content for *The Moonshot Guidebook*'s Instagram account, I decided to push past my discomfort with craft-y-ness and did a post a week for six months as I built out a physical vision board on a cork bulletin board. I'm so glad that I took on this project. It led to all kinds of discoveries for me.

In a way, I adapted part of my Pinterest methodology to the bulletin board by starting out different categories of my vision, organized around my top values printed out in 30-point font: Curiosity, Adventure, Family, Fun, Lifelong Learning, and Legacy. This proved to be extremely valuable, not only as a way to think about organizing my board but more importantly to think about and literally see how different areas of my life and vision intersect and relate with my values.

I used a mix of photos from my phone, my Pinterest board, and Google, and many of them have to do with travel. I have photos of trips I've taken with family and friends alongside photos of places around the world I hope to visit someday.

Using pictures from my life feels like a way of saying, "Yes please, more of this and this and this, thank you!" Plus using pictures from my life connects me to the memory of the exact sensations from those trips making it easy to conjure those feelings when I'm looking at those pictures of future trips.

While I still needed to fuss with printing and cutting out photos to add to the board with push pins, it was all well within my comfort zone and dare I say it, I ended up enjoying the entire project.

If you're even a hair more arts-and-crafty than me, I insist that you create a physical board. You're sure to love the process and the end result is more valuable than a digital version because it lives in your space in a way where you can see it every day.

If the idea of tinkering around with printers, poster board, or push pins sounds like too much of a hassle, I get it. Instead, check out apps like Pinterest or Canva to give yourself a digital version.

Whether you decide to go digital or tactile, don't skip this step! Try to get at least ten photos together and make a beginning habit of spending one minute each day looking at them.

Spending time each day with a visioning practice will open your mind to a whole world of opportunity.

It's too easy to let that opportunity pass by if you're being swept along in the momentum of life. Get your vision board started today!

A portion of my vision board

Get in Motion: Visioning

The main thing I always worry about when I talk to someone about visioning is that I can easily make it sound like it's some sort of big, complicated process. Let's go ahead and debunk that while we get you started on the process.

Grab yourself a notebook or a friend.

Answer the following questions, either writing your answers in a book, or bouncing back and forth between you and your friend.

1. What do I wish to learn about over the course of my life?
2. Ignoring reality (costs, the time it would take to travel, etc.), what would my perfect day be?
3. How do I wish my friends would describe me, if asked?
4. What do I wish I owned that I don't own today?
5. How would I like to be spending my time ten years from now?

That's it! That's all it takes! If you shared with a friend, I recommend spending an extra few moments getting your answers down on paper. Part of the magic of visioning is being able to return to those words over time. You reaffirm them, you change them, you live into them!

Ready to Go Further?

Here are a few recommendations for what you can do to step a little further into the practice of visioning:

- *The Moonshot Guidebook* is a workbook designed to help you find your Moonshot – that one thing you want your life to build toward, or a way to describe what life would look like if you're living your perfect day every day. Then it will help you get organized on achieving your dreams! www.moonshotguidebook.com

- Check out www.biggby.com/satellite to see the (free) intro version to the *Guidebook*. You can print it out onto a couple of sheets of paper to get started answering questions that were pulled straight out of the full-sized *Guidebook*.

- Head to www.biggby.com/visioning to check out a presentation made by *Moonshot Guidebook* co-author Laura Eich and visioning veteran and BIGGBY franchise owner Randy Neelis. They share their experience with visioning and then lead you in a brief visioning activity!

Chapter Twelve

The Power of Your Mind

This is the part of the story where I feel like brain science and the world of woo woo start to collide. The human brain has an incredible command over the body to the point where it's hard for me to avoid ascribing some level of magic power to the brain.

You've heard the stories, right? Things like the placebo effect. Athletes visualizing their performance in advance of the game and crushing it as a result. The powers of meditation. Let's dig into how some of these things work and then talk about how it relates to you living your best life.

Placebos, Nocebos, and Other Brain Trickery

I'm guessing that you've heard about the placebo effect—a phenomenon that has been observed many times while testing out new medications. One group of patients is given the new medication (the test group), another group is given a pill or injection that is only sugar or saline (the placebo group), and the final group isn't given anything (the control group). They then monitor the patients to see what they have to report. If the test group reports benefits that exceed the placebo group, the medication is deemed to be effective.

This proves to be a critical step, as a solid percentage of people who receive the placebo still feel an effect! Because they have received some level of care their belief that they should see an improvement is enough to actually experience an improvement! The placebo effect is most noticeable in cases where the medication being tested is to treat something that is subjectively measured (like pain levels), not so much when there would be an observable physical difference (reduction in the size of a tumor, for instance).

Meanwhile, there have also been studies conducted of a “nocebo” effect. Could we not have tried a titch harder on that name? Patients were given a salve to apply to a minor skin irritation caused by heat and told that it could make it better, worse, or have no effect, and sure enough, those who were told it could make things worse more often did in fact feel worse, even though it was the same salve in all cases.

In short, the power of our own beliefs can influence how we experience physical pain, for better or worse. And while we’re talking about the effects of beliefs on our physical sensations, let’s look at a few scenarios you might be familiar with.

Have you ever experienced a mosquito loose in the room? I know that when I’m hanging out in my camping hammock inside the safety of my bug net or inside my house watching TV and suddenly have that moment where I hear the vampire whine of a mosquito at my ear, unless I come away with a confirmed kill when I go to swat it away, I will spend the next half hour feeling approximately 38,000 times more itchy. Here’s what the graph would look like for the number of times the mosquito actually made contact with my skin and the number of times I thought I felt it...

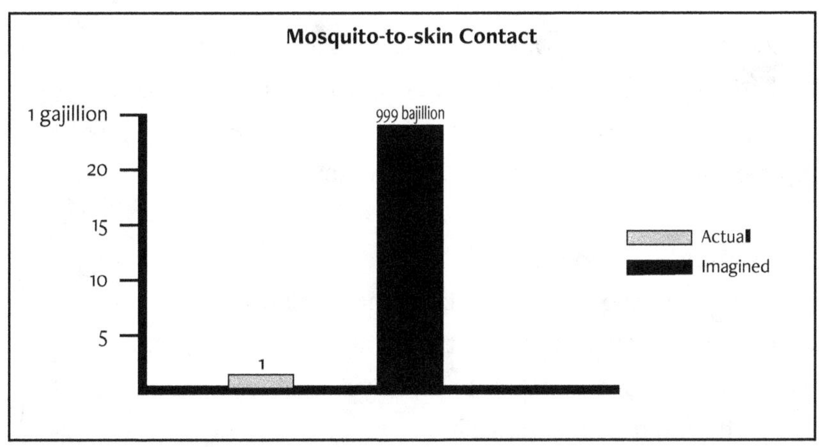

A super-fancy graph

A different scenario: Ever had the experience of talking or even just thinking about a particular dish and your mouth starts to water? If I think about biting into something sour (Sour Patch Kids being a perfect example), my salivary glands under my tongue kick into overdrive in anticipation.

Or for another example, have you ever had a physically empathetic reaction when you observe someone getting injured or perhaps even just describing an injury? I mean...America's Funniest Home Videos has made a mint off those reactions, especially the everyman hapless dad taking a whiffle ball shot straight up the middle. Whenever that type of clip aired, thousands of men across the country simultaneously and reflexively pulled their knees and thighs forward and up to shield themselves despite sitting safely at home in their living rooms. I've had the experience plenty of times where someone is describing skinning a knee or arm or coming down hard on their tail bone, and it sends an electric shiver straight up my spine.

It shouldn't come as a surprise that our thoughts can turn into physical sensations. It's that blessed lump of gray matter that's responsible for keeping your heart beating and puts one foot in front of the next when you're going for a walk. It's all connected and so much of it (thankfully) happens without you having to think about it.

Let's explore some of the ways we can take advantage of that brain-body connection to build a life we love.

Meditation is a Super Power

If you would have asked me about meditation before 2014, I would have likely waved you off, muttering about woo woo this and hippie-dippy that. Sigh. Chalk that up as yet another thing that I judged before having tried it and had it all wrong.

Meditation is a great way to get yourself acquainted with the way your mind works and also how you can better harness its power.

This was certainly true for me, in large part because outside of meditation, I spend very, very few moments across the course of the day just sitting there in silence with my own thoughts. If I'm not actively taking part in a conversation with someone, there's a close to 100 percent chance that I have something—music, podcasts, audiobooks, or TV going in the background. Whether I'm working out, getting showered and dressed, reading, writing, cooking, gardening, playing a board game, playing a video game, or going to sleep, it's almost always something. Meditating gives me a pause and some quiet moments to get my mind right at the beginning of the day.

I'm no guru, let's be clear. My first interaction with meditation was thanks to Bob, Laura, and Mike. They had attended a conference where someone had opened a session with meditation and the three of them brought that idea back to the leadership team for us to try as a way to get our minds a little clearer when we went to start off our weekly meeting.

I don't remember all of the instructions that Laura led us through back then, but I do remember enjoying the feeling of grabbing the reins of my mind and directing my attention to focus on my breathing and relaxing my muscles. Opening my eyes and blinking my way back into the space was a lovely way to gear up for the rest of our meeting. It was like being cleared for takeoff.

I would have gotten a handful of reps in at our meetings before getting inspired to try to start my day at home that way. I searched on YouTube for guided meditations and found one that I started listening to a couple of mornings a week. That meditation started with instructions for how to breathe but then took me through some visualization, asking me to picture a moment of joy and then asking me to feel the feelings I experienced in that joyful moment, ending with having me imagine that same joyful energy filling the rest of my day.

It wasn't long before I wanted to invest further in the practice, so I signed up for a subscription with Headspace, after hearing ads for it on podcasts. It really suits me, and after a little work, got it locked in as a daily habit (weekday mornings, specifically). Here's how I feel I have benefited from the nearly one thousand repetitions I have under my belt at the time of writing:

- Some meditations have asked me to focus on my breathing and then to note when a thought or feeling comes along that distracts me, to label it (e.g. to think: "that's a thought...") and then let it go, resuming my focus on my breathing. This has increased my self-awareness around my own interior monologue, making it easier to catch myself when I've gone sprinting down an unproductive mental rabbit hole and to help myself climb back out of it.
- The technique of performing a body scan, where you direct your attention from one part of your body to the next, from your feet up to the top of your head has become a use-

ful way to help me identify and relax physical stress (actual tension in the muscles) that I wasn't conscious of before starting the scan. In particular, it helped me to notice that I carry a lot of tension across my forehead and scalp. When I note it in a body scan, I feel like I'm un-scrunching the whole top of my head, bringing me a palpable sensation of relief.

- As with that first YouTube meditation, I've found that I enjoy visualization meditations the most. I love the Headspace meditation "Early Mornings," where you are directed to visualize the warmth of the sun pouring into your body and filling you, bringing a sense of energy, space, and relaxation. Which it actually does for me! I think about being out on "the back 40,"—aka the part of our four acres that is my personal nature retreat—tilting my head back to bring the sun full onto my face and start to sense that kind of warmth and brightness, filling from my toes up.

It was a powerful feeling, especially at first, to realize that my mind could actually conjure that kind of sensation in my body. It told me that there was a lot more that I might be able to do that I hadn't considered before. A little bit like that scene that's so typical of superhero movies, where they first realize that they have a hidden power and it quickly becomes "let's see what else I can do!" This was the moment that meditation got especially good for me.

Like those superhero movies, I recommend you go through your own heroic meditation training montage...the first scenes of which you might throw your hands up after a few minutes of your mind continuing to race away from you while you tried to focus on the guided meditation, followed by a another of your eyes closed, a sense of calm spreading across your features only to be interrupted by some sort of household hijinks (this happens to me—Izzy always seems to get thirsty in the middle of my meditation, loudly slurping from her bowl), to another scene of you breathing slowly and evenly, and so on.

Our brains are powerful devices and meditation is just one of the ways you can start to harness that power. It is a practice however. Meaning that you might think "meditation isn't for me" when what you really need is to give it time and build up some repetitions. Practice flying all you want—it's an awesome super power too—but building up a solid meditation practice might be a wee bit more easily achieved.

Visualizing Like a Champ

In chapter 11, we talked about the power of visioning. I skipped a crucial detail in the brain science of it all that we still need to cover. Let's talk about our incredible power of visual perception and its close cerebral cousin, mental imagery.

Our power of visual perception is the primary way that we humans make sense of our world. "Primary" in that it comes first. It is the sense that aids us at the greatest distance to help make sense of the world around us. Unless something has gone horribly wrong, you'll not be feeling, tasting, smelling, or hearing that mountain range on the horizon. We have more brain real estate dedicated to our vision than our other senses.

The parts of the cerebral cortex that are responsible for interpreting the sensory input that hits our retinas help us to sort our world by color, shape, texture, movement, depth of field and so on. That exact same neighborhood in the brain also goes to work when you are consciously putting together a mental image (a different area is responsible for all the wacky stuff when you're asleep and dreaming).

And while mental imagery is always a fuzzier, less distinct image than your visual perception, picturing things in your mind can set off dominos in the other parts of your brain almost as if it's happening in real life. And those dominos? They're capable of setting off all kinds of cool responses in your real life if you start to use them intentionally by practicing visualization.

Visualization, as you might guess from the name, can come into play as you do visioning work and for sure with vision boards. But before we get to that, let's talk about the dominos tipping their way toward awesomeness as they work their way across your brain and into your life.

Athletes have frequently testified to the power of visualization improving their performance on the field.

We can talk about Olympic swimmer Michael Phelps (you know, only the most decorated Olympian in history, with 28 total medals). Along with the countless hours of physical training that Michael put in on his way to becoming the champion that he is, he also spent hours and hours, ever since he was a teenager, practicing his mental game. His coach and his mom helped him learn a relaxation routine as well as a visualization practice to help him prepare for his meets. He would think through all the steps involved in the process, including what could go wrong and how he would react, as well as what a perfect swim would look like. He was able to step up on the block, be loose and relaxed, and having rehearsed this moment many, many times in real life and mentally, when he leapt from the block, he was on Automatic Crush It mode.

Beyond Phelps, go ahead and add Katie Ledecky (another gold medalist and world record swimmer) and Lindsey Vonn (gold medalist and World Cup downhill skier) to the list of Olympians who are proponents of visualization. Oh, right, and just about every other Olympic athlete: A study showed that 90% of Olympians surveyed used some form of visualization with 97% of them saying they believed it helped their performance.

Let's dig into what happens inside the brain when you do visualization. This can work for anyone doing any kind of visualization, but I think it's especially going to be effective for athletes or others who are visualizing physical activity where response time is an important factor.

The Air Traffic Controller in Your Brain

Our brains have a little nugget in them that's called the reticular activating system (RAS). It's responsible for helping us focus on important details and to filter out all of the unimportant sensory input.

It's like the air traffic controller of your brain keeping track of all the sights, sounds, smells, textures, tastes and the less famous senses like nociception (responsible for you jerking your hand away from a hot surface before you've even consciously realized it's hot) and proprioception (it helps you know which way is up). You have sensory stimuli flying through your nervous system constantly and your little RAS brain nugget is keeping track of all of them and letting them know which senses are approved to come in for a landing in the front of your conscious brain.

This air traffic controller is super good at its job. Even if you consider yourself a distractible person, I promise you that you are filtering out an immense amount of stimuli moment by moment by moment.

For example, as I sit here typing this, let me try to dial into only the sound stimuli that are available to me if I were to pay attention: I have music playing in the room with me, the keyboard does its clicky clack in response to my work, I can hear the background out-in-the-country noise of the crickets and frogs singing away looking for love outside my cracked window, the shuff shuff of my hands and wrists passing across the felt fabric that they rest on as I type, my dog licking (Ew! What is she licking?), those random house creaks that happen from time to time, the muffled sound of my wife watching TV up in bed, my other dog sniffing at the cracked window, the jingle of her collar, and if I pause my music, a distant dog bark, a car speeding up through its gears as it passes our private drive on the nearby road, and the quiet oooooooooooff of air coming through the vents from the fans in our HVAC system.

Now you play. This time, dial into your sense of touch. What sensations come through now that I've asked you? If you're seated or lying down, how many different points of contact can you detect? Can you feel your clothing on you now? Can you feel air moving against your skin?

How many of those sensations were you aware of before I directed your attention there? My guess is probably very, very few, in the same way that before I paused to listen, I was only really occasionally noticing my music playing and my dog's self-care routine when it got especially...vigorous.

Our air traffic controller is an expert! But as you saw with my examples, it can be directed, even tricked, to give some sensory input preferential treatment, allowing it to get through the filter, and, in some cases, get through it fast.

Athletes who visualize their performance are training their reticular activating system, as if they're showing their air traffic controller a slideshow of the planes they expect to see come in later that day. That visualization work strengthens connections throughout the brain that allows the athletes to decrease their reaction times—just imagine how much of an advantage shaving a few fractions of a second could create when making the turn in the pool, the cut on the ski slope, or edging out the goalie on a shot.

This kind of mental rehearsal can also help pre-load responses to adverse conditions. A player might spend time doing visualization around how they would respond to a referee making a bad call on a play that they're in. The natural reaction for a player in that situation might be surprise, outrage, or anger directed back at the ref. But what would the best reaction be? What sort of reaction would meet the intersection of the player being their best self and create the sort of response in the ref that might benefit the player and their team later in the game? The player can't know whether this situation will present itself with the ref making the bad call, but if it does, and they've spent time getting mental rehearsals in, they have a much-improved chance of showing up as their best self to get best results because they've preloaded their response.

Rehearsals for Your Dream Life

Let's take it back to visioning and vision boards. When we take the time to write down details of what we want our future life to look like, we are playing in the exact same playground where athletes are doing their visualization work. This is why it's particularly important to write down visually descriptive details, creating a mental image of the outcomes you want. It's also why it's important to continue coming back to these visions repeatedly, like a mental rehearsal for your future life.

That's one of the reasons I love using *The Moonshot Guidebook*–it has helped me to develop and then revisit and reevaluate my dreams. By the end of your first year using the Guidebook, you will have written down your Moonshot 10 different times and written out dozens of supporting details of what your life will look like having achieved your Moonshot. Repetition is key to developing a rich and detailed vision for your life.

Those details, which we call a Lunar Landscape, provide you with the opportunity to build a rewarding visualization practice for your life. The beginning of my current Lunar Landscape looks like this:

I've recently started a new daily practice of spending a few moments each morning visualizing these scenes. This is another part of my morning routine, following meditation, gratitude, and affirmations. I close my eyes, and then one by one picture each future scene, doing five of the 10 one day, then the other five the next day, and repeat.

So, for example, my first item on the list reads like a picture of Megan and me walking our dogs around Holyrood Park in Edinburgh, Scotland (we dream of living part of the year there in our retirement). When I visualize it, it's more like a micro-movie. I picture the two of us, gray haired, wrinkles telling the story of our age, a twinkle in our eyes, holding hands, she on the left, me on the right, walking a respectable but measured pace. We chat and we laugh, at each other and our dogs, both small pups, girls, as we've always had, one a lab mix, and the other a cute but hard-to-identify mutt. The grassy hill of Arthur's Seat dominates the middle of the park, sloped as if bowing in deference to the nearby castle. We hear wisps of rich Scottish brogue from the people we pass by, punctuated with the occasional accent of a person who, like us, might now call Edinburgh home. The air is slightly cool, but the sun warms my skin.

Are you there with me? Can you picture the scene? Now that particular scene may not light up every joyful neuron in your brain, but holy cow does that ever fill me up with warm light. That's the first

achieved it? You will continue to refine these details in Session Two, so don't agonize!

1] Megan and me, old and cute and holding hands, walking our dogs, loose-leash beside us, as we stroll around Holyrood Park.
2] Me on the oversized screen porch of our tiny home, reading, dog at my side, steam rising from my tea - Megan and another dog napping inside.
3] Family and friends sitting around our dinner table, chatting and laughing, and I bring food to the table - something delicious and comforting, my own recipe.
4] A barista who I never met, sharing her moonshot with her employees at her own company, at their holiday party, as she passes out their free Guidebook copies for next year.
5] Me on stage, sharing how BIGGBY transformed into a purpose-driven learning culture across all its franchises - the audience is smiling & leaning in.
6] Megan, me, Mak & J&M, having dinner outside, mountains visible in the background.

My Lunar Landscape, January 2024

of five I do to start my day. It's like the right side of my brain giving the left side a hug each morning. It's a perfect way to get all my good brain chemicals going and then, meanwhile, I've given my reticular activating system a treasure map to my future joy. Do you think there's any chance that I'd unconsciously ignore any opportunities that connect to that possible future? Yeah, no. I am dialed in.

What about you? What scene would you picture? Are you on a beach somewhere? At a ball game in the front row? In the back of house working the line in your own restaurant? Old and brimming with joy, surrounded by grandkids and great grandkids? Taking in the sunset from the deck of your lake house?

Whatever that scene is, I want you to take one minute to visualize the scene. Close your eyes and picture what you see, imagine what you hear, smell, feel, and taste. Set a timer and enjoy yourself.

Sink into the reality of your dream for your future.

No really, I want you to do this right now. I'll wait!

...

How did that go for you? Were you able to connect to that dream with more than one of your senses? How did that make you feel?

If that was your first try at taking an intentional moment to picture that scene, I promise that if you make a habit of doing that once a day every day, you will build up an enthralling mental image of your dream in very short order.

And let's not forget about vision boards! There's a reason why they're a dashboard to your dreams. If you were to build a practice of scanning across all of the images and words on your board each morning, you're doing the same thing: brain training. Juicing up your brain with all those positive energy chemicals.

To me, it's kind of like scanning past the thumbnails of movies on a streaming service. One little image of a movie that's familiar to you can conjure a whole raft of memory and emotions. And like you would on Netflix, I recommend you "click" on one of those favorites from time to time to get the full experience. Rather than just looking at the images and acknowledging them, do a full visualization, pulling yourself into that picture. Experiencing it through all of your senses.

Get in Motion: Start Your Vision Board

That's now two successive chapters where I've talked about vision boards. Listen, I wasn't into this idea to begin with, but it turned out that it was fun to put together and is a sneaky effective way of tricking your brain into spotting opportunities in your life that let you reach your dreams! All of that to say, this is going to be worth it, so let's dig in!

Your First Ten Pictures

I'm going to help you select your first 10 pictures for your vision board. It will be up to you to decide whether you end up printing these out to go onto a cork board or poster board or whether they stay in the digital space for you. Wherever they end up, just make sure you get them in front of you regularly! Get out your phone and let's get started!

Whether in your photos, social media, or by googling, find a picture of...

1. You, where you were completely happy, filled with a kind of excitement.
2. You, where you were completely happy, filled with a sense of contentment.
3. Someone who inspires you, whether you know them personally or not.

4. A place you would travel to if money wasn't an issue.
5. A feeling you want more of in your life...Google it and find an image that speaks to you.
6. A hobby or skill you wish you had.
7. Your dream home, whether that's actually a house, condo, school bus refitted as a RV, etc.
8. A challenge you want to take on some day, in your own life or for the world.
9. Something that represents what you want to be doing or have done a year from now.
10. Something that represents how you want to be spending your time 10 years from now.

If any of these prompts draws a complete blank for you, that's zero percent a problem! These were all written from my perspective, so if one or more don't fit for you, that's to be expected—you're a completely different human being than me! Instead, either double up on another prompt or just go in search of other pictures that bring you a sense of hope, inspiration, or joy!

VISION

Chapter 13

How Do You Want to Be?

Before we started to delve into self-awareness work at BIGGBY, I didn't give much thought at all about what kind of person I could be. The closest I would have come before that was to have (plenty of) ideas about how I might be differently shaped, and what kind of work would go into that. Zero-point-zero percent dedicated to how I might change the way I behaved toward the people around me.

It's at least a little embarrassing to consider, looking back. Let's take stock of where I was as a thirty-something, prior to these revelations. I would have been thriving in my career, married happily for several years, a dog dad a couple times over, and completely ignorant of the idea that I have the ability to choose how I want to be as a person. Nothing wrong with that, right? All good, but I didn't know how much I was missing, asleep in the back seat of my life.

When we began to explore things like *Strengthsfinder* and the DiSC Assessment, I began to better understand who I am, what my strengths are, and what it might look like when I'm deep in a blind spot (spoiler: it's not pretty).

Because I better understand my natural tendencies, I now have an opportunity to actually catch myself in those old blind spots. By taking those personality tests, reading through the results, talking about them with the people around me, it's like I've installed a little side view mirror on the front of my brain. I might not always remember to check it, but when I do, I can see into my blind spot in a way that saves me a lot of trouble.

Learning how you behave when you're in a blind spot is not fun. In fact, it's kinda' the opposite. It's a little bit like going out on a series of dates with the nightmare version of yourself, learning a bit more about them, one awkward conversation after the next.

I guess within the context of that metaphor, that makes me your chaperone. I suppose that's a little weird, but I promise that I'll pick good music for the car. Anyway, let's get going and see what comes up for you...

Clarity from Common Language

Somewhere in 2014 or '15 I read *Now, Discover Your Strengths.* The book is based on a ton of research by Gallup, and, in recent years, has been reimagined as *Strengthsfinder 2.0.* The book comes with an access code for a short personality test (or you can skip the book and just pay for the test and read about your results in the Gallup app). At the end of the process, you'll be given a list of your top five strengths.

The premise of the book is that too often in life in the United States, we are operating in a frame of "fix yourself." Measure the ways that you are not enough and then do all the work you have to (and buy all the things you need to) in order to improve yourself.

This starts in school where grades start from A-plus or 4.0 perfect score and then count backward to an F or 0.0. Every mistake counts against us. It's not the progress that we make that gets recognized, nor is it the skills we have in spades that aren't being measured by the particular test at hand.

The book makes the point that we all have inherent gifts and that we're all better off if we can keep ourselves focused on maximizing those strengths rather than trying to shore up all our shaky weaknesses.

When I first took the *Strengthsfinder* test, these were my top five:

1. Strategic
2. Achiever
3. Competition
4. Input
5. Analytical

Getting my results was like...check, check, check, check, and check. They all made perfect sense to me. I ended up doing a deep dive on the content. I was Director of Operations at the time, and I worked to memorize everyone's top five strengths in my department. I felt that it could help me to better understand what motivates people and could indicate what lens they might be looking through that informed their perspective on the world.

Our Operations Manager was my right hand. We worked together closely on all things operations and training, and just as I thought my top five strengths were spot on, I thought the same for hers as well. Consistency was in her top five. Strategic was my number 1. And that difference was the dynamic that put the two of us into conflict more than anything else.

People blessed with Consistency have a real drive to establish rules that everyone can abide by, and have a strong desire for everyone to play by the same rules. No exceptions or special treatment, everyone is equal. She was awesome as a rules enforcer. She never hesitated to step up and tell someone they needed to shape up.

Me, on the other hand, I was too much of a people pleaser to be able to do that effortlessly. Beyond that, my Strategic strength was often calling me to look at an issue from multiple sides and see if there might not be a better way to arrange things long term. My hesitation to enforce a rule if I saw a stronger benefit in the bigger picture drove her crazy. I was impressed by her desire to keep people in line but when I thought she was throwing out the long-term-strategic-win baby with the short-term-consistent-treatment bath water it made me bonkers.

Because *Strengthsfinder* provided us with a common language, it made it much easier for us to be able to see things from each other's perspectives. Before that time, I would have been much more likely to simply describe her as capital-W WRONG, but after, I was better able to appreciate that she was coming from a different perspective that had real strength of character behind it.

When we'd find ourselves suddenly toe to toe and getting a little red-faced about which course of action to take, it became a prompt for us to pause and zoom out for a moment to see not just what we were arguing about, but how we were looking at the situation. Understanding each others' strengths and having a common language to describe them consistently provided us better results (see what I did there?).

While *Strengthsfinder* happened to be my pathway into the insight about the value of common language, you can get that value out of any personality test (refer back to chapter 6 for some of my fave personality tests). The most important thing is that you involve the people around you. It's only once you and your people have a shared understanding of each other in the context of the personality test's terminology that you'll begin reaping the benefits of those shortcuts.

An Achiever Wrestles with Himself at the Riverside

As I gave additional thought to each of my top strengths and how they benefited me, it also invited me to consider what it looked like when those strengths took over the show, but instead to my detriment. As an example of what that looks like, let's talk about my Achiever strength.

As a strength, my Achiever does a ton of good work for me. I consider it one of my defining characteristics. I am driven by getting things done. I love a good To Do list, and if I get my teeth into a project I can enter into a state of flow where I just want to keep going and going and going until I get it done.

However. It also means that I can struggle to just relax and "do nothing." It means that I can overwork and get myself burned out. Because I put more value in the getting-things-done I can undervalue simply...being.

My wife is not an Achiever. I'm not saying that she hasn't accomplished great things. I'm not saying that she isn't a hard worker. But she does know how to call it quits. She does know how to just enjoy being. She's perfectly content for us to snuggle up and pass half a day binging a TV show. I'm perfectly content to watch one episode. I'm pretty good with watching a second episode. I'm coming out of my skin to watch a third episode if I have other things that "need" doing.

It means that if I accomplish a whole bunch but fall short of my goal, I can walk away feeling like a loser. Fun fact, I'm struggling against that very thing right this moment as I type this.

I've taken the day off of work today, a Friday. It's a perfect Michigan fall day, with temps moving between the 40s and the 60s. I had set a goal for myself to write for three hours at a stretch today. Previously, the most I'd ever written for this book was an hour in a single sitting. I had an awesome morning, getting all kinds of good work done on a game I'm developing, went out for a nice lunch while working on prepping for a meeting I'm hosting on Monday, and hiked out into the woods to set up my hammock alongside the Thornapple River, cool air and birdsong enveloping me.

It's been 2 hours and 10 minutes and I'm kinda' ready to be done. I'm still getting good work done, but Megan will be getting home from work soon and I'm just not sure that it's the biggest best thing for me to hang out here for another hour-ish just because I said I would. I think it might be nice to settle into our weekend a bit early and get together our dinner plans. I've more than doubled my previous record for length of time writing, but because I have this three-hour goal, if I pack it in now, I'm going to be disappointed in myself and risk not being able to feel present and joyful to head into the weekend and hang with Megan.

Stupid Achiever. But do you see how this works? Can you relate? What are your strengths and what are the attendant blind spots to them? Are you highly adaptable but also a bit of a pushover? Are you grounded in a set of beliefs about how the world works but meanwhile a bit intolerant toward other perspectives? Do you love to get into the details and sort through what might be the best option, but at the same time are prone to indecision and slow action?

Learn what your strengths are and how, when overused, they become weaknesses.

Whether working solo or in a team setting, being clear about both sides of your strengths makes you more effective.

And in case you're wondering: Yes, yes I did stay for the full three hours. And not a minute more.

At the riverside, mid-struggle

Best Self

Imagine a moment where you are able to put your strengths to use while doing something that fulfills you. You are not being hampered by any of your weaknesses nor are you caught in a blind spot. It's the kind of moment where you can actually get present to the feeling of being the very best version of you. Just picture basking in that sensation.

It's an incredibly rewarding feeling and I'm fortunate because I've reached a place in my life where parts of my job give me those opportunities regularly. Most often it comes after I've wrapped up a coaching session where the coachee had something that they wanted to go to work on and I was able to bring parts of my experience to bear in a way that helps me ask just the right question that opens up a new perspective for them or where they walk away knowing exactly what they want to do next.

I leave those sessions feeling fully alive, buzzing with energy. So much so that sometimes I have to let it out by getting up from my desk, walking around my house, making a bunch of silly happy noises at my dogs. Picture me, babbling a pidgin language of part-turkey, part-Muppet, through a full smile at my dogs, blinking up at me from their latest nap.

So why then, don't I just go and be my best self in every single coaching session so I can feel that way all the time?

Yeah, no, it doesn't work like that. There are plenty of sessions that I do that are perfectly lovely. I might be able to help a little here or there, but because of where the coachee was, and what they needed that day, it doesn't hit a full BINGO for me. Other times I'm sure I fall short for both of us because I allowed myself to get pulled into a blind spot, or the coachee might have been in a place where, if I would have had a different set of strengths, they would have gotten exactly what they needed, but with me that day, it might just end up being a solid B for them, solid and all, but not that A-plus feeling.

Me getting pulled into a blind spot would look like me getting into problem solving mode, a natural part of my disposition, when what the person really needed was lots of empathy, a chance to know that they've really been heard and that they're not alone. This is sort of like having a friend who's assembling a piece of furniture and you show up to help armed with a hammer when what they really could have used was another Allen wrench. Like: "Cool buddy. I appreciate the intent to help, but this isn't going to do it for me."

It's not that I lack empathy! But it's definitely not one of those always-at-hand, top five strengths, where it's always right there in my tool belt ready to go. That's why I am working on developing a stronger sense of empathy. I know that there is opportunity for growth. But I also know that it will never be as strong a trait for me as it is for someone like my friend and teammate Alisha.

Alisha is the friend who I go to when (whether consciously or not) I'm looking for someone to be 100 percent on my side. Not looking for questioning, or challenging, or problem-solving. In those moments I choose Alisha because I just want to bask in the warm glow of her personality. It's not that she can't question, challenge, or problem-solve, but those aren't her natural go-to ways of being. But she's brilliant at being there with you, feeling your feelings, and then putting her positivity to work (another trait that is not a top strength for me) to make you feel like you've got this, you can do it, go out there and get it!

Working inside *The Moonshot Guidebook* is what got me to thinking about wanting to further develop my ability to be empathetic. There is a section in it called the Flight Plan. It presents you with a series of questions, asking you to reflect on your strengths and your opportunities for growth. One of the questions has you write out your top five strengths, explaining what they mean to you, and then to write out what you wish your top ten strengths would be, including an encouragement to rearrange any of your top five as you do.

I love this activity. It helps me to think about how I use my strengths in my daily life and what more I could do if I could cultivate my strengths. While working through the activity, looking at the list of strengths, I thought about how being more empathetic could make me a more effective coach. I wrote it in as my fifth strength on the list of ten.

Writing that down in my Flight Plan worksheet did the thing that visioning work tends to do: It helped me to see opportunity. While reading *Dare to Lead*, by Brené Brown, I locked onto a perfectly concise metaphor that describes the difference between empathy and sympathy. I spent a lifetime up until that moment getting confused about the distinction between the two.

In the book, Brown writes: "Empathy fuels connection. Sympathy drives disconnection." She then describes someone who fell down a well. The empathetic passerby sees them and climbs down to be with them and then help them get out. The sympathetic person who passes by the well looks down and says, "Oh, that looks awful. So sorry for your trouble," and then continues about their business. I love this description. It's visually powerful, which makes it easier to remember, but it also feels to me like a simple instruction manual for how to be empathetic.

Now when a coachee is describing a situation, I think to myself, "Climb down into the well with them!" Even though I'm sure I'd heard the description of empathy as "putting yourself in the other person's shoes" countless times across my life, it was Brown's description of the well that has actually helped me to step into them. I listen to what the coachee is saying and picture how I would feel if I was right there with them, right down in that well.

Now I can say back to them things like: "I know that can feel really scary, how are you feeling about it?" or "That's really crummy, that would hurt my feelings and I think I would feel betrayed. What has it been like for you?" My aim, by articulating my empathetic feeling for where they are at and then asking them what it's actually like, is to create a little more safe space in the conversation to let them know that I'm trying to understand and that those big feelings, if they have them, are okay.

It is still a calculated step for me; it's not second-nature, like it would be for Alisha. But it feels right to me because I know it's helping me to grow, and most often it deepens the conversation I'm having with the other person, whether that's a coachee, a friend, or Megan.

This is the value of measuring your day-to-day ordinary self against the very best version of you.

Seeing that best version of yourself lets you know what you're capable of when you're feeling and behaving at your absolute peak.

Contrasting your best self with how you go through the average day can highlight where you have opportunity to grow. It lets you into consider how you want to be as a person.

How do you feel and what do you do when you're at your best? And where are the gaps between best you and average you? How can you focus on one of those areas to hit best-self-ness more consistently?

Worst Self

Where there's a best, a worst is sure to be lurking nearby.

This one won't require an exercise for you to figure out. I'm guessing that you might also be familiar with what it looks like to be your worst self. I'm sorry if that's the case, but I can, you know, empathize.

Your worst self might show up when you've acted out from a place of fear. It might be because you feel isolated, ignored, or shamed. It could come from a place of envy or jealousy. Maybe from seeking retribution for a perceived wrong?

Whatever the cause, your worst self showed up and behaved terribly, lashing out in a feeble attempt to reestablish things the way you wish they were.

Does any of that sound familiar to you? What does your worst self look like? How do you behave?

I've had plenty of times where I've shown up as my worst self. Petty. Vindictive. Sniping. Fighting for attention. Trying to outdo others and leave them behind. Alllllll of that gross stuff. My wife, being the human who gets to spend the most time with me, has seen me in Ugly Mode more than anyone else.

Megan has surely seen me at my worst. Most often, when it's bad for me, like for all of us, it's not me at my absolute worst. It's me at a C-minus. Like, I'm here, I'm doing it, but I'm kind of sucking at it in a way that isn't inspiring anyone, least of all me.

For me, C-minus is going to look like either Not Trying or Returning Fire.

Not Trying Jeremy is the guy who lets his wife do the majority of care for our pups. He's the one who neglects the house cleaning that he knows needs to get done until Megan marshals us both into action. Not Trying Jeremy lets Megan do all the planning for us socially.

Returning Fire Jeremy is the aggrieved spouse who, whether Megan was at all upset with me, will feel wounded by a comment and rather than absorb it from a place of peace and wisdom and ask what's going on and how can I help (like Patrick, my emotional role model, would do), instead, Returning Fire Jeremy gets super petty and snide and makes that wisecrack that's meant to both cut deep and also give me a mealy-mouthed escape route to claim that I didn't mean it.

Yuck. Just yuck. Just look at that guy. Ew. But yeah, that's me at times. Really more of a D- than a C-minus, right? It's not who I'm trying to be. It's not me most of the time. But do I end up there in my weak moments? Where I'm tired or afraid or insecure? Yep, yep, and yep.

But I'm also familiar with what I look like when I'm at my best. I can be a harbor in a storm for people. I tend to be even-keeled, so if a person is just having a terrible go of it and is upset, terribly sad, or freaking out, when they land with me, I will make it better. I might not be able to fix anything, but I can give them the calm, collected me, make sure they know that they are loved and important and that I'll do anything I can to see them through it. I can be thoughtful, bringing extra perspective or insight into a conversation, or be the person to reach out to you to express some gratitude when you might not have expected it. I can be full of ideas and inspiration and communicate all of it in a way that helps you become a part of it and motivate you to action. I can be tender, caring, and understanding. That's all A-plus Jeremy.

Megan also gets to experience this version of me more than

anyone, a small benefit that I hope outweighs the nastiness and disappointment of C-minus Jeremy.

What do you look like, talk like, sound like, and feel like when you're at your very best and at your very worst? What do you look like when you're at a solid C-minus?

This is important to grapple with because they're all you! You bring all of that to the table. And you also have more choice in the matter than what you might think, especially in the moment.

This takes us back, in some ways, to what I talked about in A-Hole to Hospital in chapter 4. We cannot, in any way, control the world around us. We can influence a little of it, but control? We can only hope to control ourselves. We always have a choice about how to react to a circumstance, even if it doesn't feel like it. Who do you want to show up each time? Your best self, or the schlocky jerk version of yourself?

It's your best self, right? Even when you are confronted with a world-class butthead, you know that you showing up as your worst self won't help matters, especially over the long run. As the saying goes, two world-class buttheads don't make a right.

If you want to always show up as your best self, what's getting in the way?

Oh, right. A lifetime worth of experiences that have shaped the contours of your brain.

You have created a whole machine of a system in your brain to operate just so. It is a fine-tuned and whirring factory with automated assembly lines taking in stimuli and churning out responses. These products have come off your neural assembly line thousands and thousands of times. Now, when you want to change things, it's just like an employee on the floor at a plant hitting the big red stop button. It's going to cause a certain amount of problems to get things straightened out and moving again with a fix in place.

The best shot that you have is to get other people involved. Until you've been given a fair amount of practice at spotting yourself in a blind spot, the people around you will be the best qualified to help you hit that Stop button on the assembly lines you have that crank out nasty reflexes.

The Bossy Finger

The most powerful and ultimately effective experience I've had with receiving outside support came from an ungraceful moment that I had with a bunch of people who I love and respect.

This was in the summer of 2018, shortly after my move to the BOOST Sphere. Laura and I were facilitating the launch of a new Leadership Forum. We were on day two of the launch, which follows the traditional first day spent out in the woods. Day two is where the group works to decide what they're going to be about, as a group, across their first year of existence.

It was nearing the scheduled end of the day, and I was functioning as the administrator, helping keep track of the decisions they had made and taking notes as they went. I was doing my very best to keep up throughout the flurry of decisions that were coming together as the meeting was coming to its close and at one point, as a group member was making a new proposal to the group for another detail of how they would operate, I threw my pointer finger in the air, with a bossy and grumpy "Wait, wait, wait" type attitude. The moment passed without commentary from the group, I caught up in my notes, and things proceeded.

But later that afternoon, after the Forum members said their goodbyes and got on the road to head home, Laura asked if we could debrief the day. I'm sure we talked about how proud we were of the group and how well they came together and expressed appreciation for things that each of us did along the way during the day to help make that happen. I don't remember those parts of the conversation specifically. I do remember Laura asking about that bossy, grumpy finger I threw into the air.

I remember it because the series of questions she asked me put me on a path to greater self-awareness around one aspect of how I'm built that I previously hadn't given any thought to. She said, "Do you remember that moment, with the finger?" while doing an extra-dramatized sassy finger wave in my face. "What was that about? That was super out of character for you, and it changed the energy in the room for a minute."

I had to really think about it to make sure I knew what she was talking about—this is the nature of a blind spot. I was so focused on accomplishing the task at hand (a strength of mine) that I had completely blocked out anyone else's needs (the blind spot).

Once I knew for sure what Laura was referring to, I told her "I knew that we were getting into a time crunch to get everything we needed to get finished, and I was struggling to keep up, so I was feeling a lot of pressure in the moment." She nodded and then asked the key question that sent me off on my self-awareness journey: "What did you actually feel inside you in the moment?" She gestured across herself, prompting me to consider what sensations I would have been feeling across my body at the moment the bossy finger came out.

I pictured myself back in the moment and thought about that sense of being under pressure and realized that it was a distinct feeling that I'd had at the time: a sense of tightness, right around my solar plexus. This became a real gift to me, this moment. Laura had given me a key to unlock a little bit more self-awareness; something I could use to improve how I work with others.

I learned in that moment that I have a signal my body sends me when I'm feeling under pressure about time, something I could try to catch happening in real time. And sure enough, that's how it played out for me. The nature of my job is to be in a lot of meetings, so I had plenty of opportunities to practice.

To be clear, I don't get anxious near the close of every meeting, thank goodness. It's specifically meetings where we're trying to arrive at a certain outcome where it presents the possibility that I'll feel that time pressure. Today, 90 percent of the time, I stay out of my blind spot. I might not notice right away, kinda' in the same way I don't notice the precise moment a headache starts, but rather it's a slower dawning awareness. But usually, within a few minutes, I'll become aware that I've got that feeling in my chest and it snaps me back awake—I'm no longer in the feeling of pressure, I'm able to observe that I'm feeling that way, note it, and by doing that, it gives me an extra measure of control to watch out for how I'm behaving with the people around me.

I still feel pressured. That part doesn't go away. Whatever the thing is that's deep inside me that really really cares about doing the thing we said we're going to do and really cares about getting out on time, that part of me is still ringing the alarm bell. And 10 percent of the time I get swept up by that sensation and can find myself behaving badly as a result. But because of that little gift of self-awareness Laura granted me with her question, ninety percent of the time I have a chance to intervene before the bossy finger comes out. I get to ask myself:

How do you want to be?

It means the difference between me regularly showing up as another version of me at a C-minus—let's call him Aggrieved Jeremy—and having the opportunity to show up for people around me as my very best self.

I grew up not knowing that I had a choice about how I want to be as a person. I was just Default Jeremy all the time. But now I know I have a choice: I can cultivate my strengths and grow my self-awareness so that I can avoid all those C-minus Jeremy blind spots. I want to be my best self.

Get in Motion: How Do You Want to Be?

Whether it's from taking stock of your strengths, receiving feedback about your blind spots, or from wanting to show up as your best self, let's get a picture of how you want to be as a person and then determine what kind of support you could use from the people around you to help you get there.

Get out your notebook or grab a friend to work through these questions!

Building the Picture

1. What would I hope my friends would say about me if someone asked?
2. What are my strengths?
3. What would it look like for me to overuse those strengths in a way where I'm in a blind spot?
4. What are the things that the people in my life know they can rely on me for?
5. What interpersonal activities or interactions leave me feeling the best? What am I doing and thinking about in those moments when they're happening?
6. How do I act when I'm a solid C-minus?
7. How do I act when I'm my worst self?

8. Based on everything above, how do I want to be as a person? Don't describe what you don't want to be; so, if you don't want to be angry, for example, what characteristic do you want to embody instead?

Getting Support

If you're fortunate, you have people who love you enough to call you out. They might be the type of people who tell you if you have something in your teeth or the type who lovingly tell you that you are being a jerk when that kind of feedback saves you from backsliding from your C-minus self to your very worst self. These are the people you will need to engage to get the most out of this part of the activity.

9. What blind spot (from #3 above) would benefit me the most to be able to disrupt?
10. If someone were to point it out to me, which blind spot behaviors could I stop in the moment?
11. Based on what I said for #6 above, what could a loved one say to me to help me snap out of the mental space that contributes to C-Minus Me?
12. How could a loved one help me before or even after I've become the worst version of me?

Chapter Fourteen

What Do You Want to Do?

"What do you want to be when you grow up?" I wonder how many kids grow up with that question rattling around in their brains in search of a solid answer?

As a little kid, I was fascinated with police and firefighters. My dad was the mayor of our city. In case you harbor the same question that many of my elementary school peers did: No, no, this did not mean that I got to ride around in a limo. It did mean that we got to ride in the Fourth of July parade in a fancy classic car. I didn't care about the car, but throwing candy and waving was fun. That privilege didn't come anywhere close to counterbalancing the other side effect of being the mayor's kid, though—standing around, b-o-r-e-d, waiting for dad to finish talking to someone he bumped into while we were running errands. This happened everywhere, all the time.

But another small privilege was being able to run amok around city hall, including getting to talk to police officers and working out in their gym in the basement of the building. We also knew the fire chief, who lived in our neighborhood. I remember being curious about all the trappings of being a fire fighter.

So maybe when I was little, if asked, “What do you want to be when you grow up?” I might have responded with “A policeman, or maybe a firefighter!” Something with lights and sirens (which was easily the central attraction)! Or maybe I would have said I wanted to be an astronaut, on the strength of the dehydrated “astronaut ice cream” that seemed to be sold at every museum gift shop when I was growing up.

You might not be surprised to find that I abandoned those career paths before doing a thing to work toward them. I also notice that there aren’t a lot of princesses and NBA players around. It just might be that dreaming is the easy part.

As I grew up, I remember also having a brief period where I wanted to be an architect (literally no idea how that one got in there... maybe because I liked to draw as a kid?) and a longer period of being interested in becoming a marine biologist. That one is easy to explain. The summer before middle school we moved to a house on a lake, and I spent my summers on and in that lake.

So, I definitely grew up with having at least a dream or two rattling around in my head. I think the marine biologist one died when I started having to consider that it would probably mean having to relocate to one of the coasts and leaving my family, which was a no-go as far as I was concerned.

Do you recall being asked when you were a kid what you wanted to be when you grew up? I would bet that you did. Like me, did you shuffle through a handful of those dreams before you made it to high school? And perhaps landed nowhere near any of those particular dreams when you started adulting your way into your first career path?

Welcome to the 94 percent majority. According to a study that followed kids into adulthood, it’s just a narrow six percent of folks who stay on the career path they set as a childhood aspiration.

For those who head on to college, a change of direction is common there too. A quick Google search tells me that 70-80 percent of undergraduate students end up changing majors. Makes sense to me. Everyone is just trying to figure themselves out, so changing course (and college courses, for that matter) feels like a natural consequence.

So if you, like me, have zig zagged your way around trying to find a sense of direction, like one of those ole' timey fellas with the Y-shaped stick looking for water, you've got all kinds of good company.

We'll get into the pros and cons of staying the course and of changing your direction. You'll see that I don't think there's a single right answer. Then we'll talk about the connection between lifestyle choices we make, our paychecks, and the cost of our own time.

Finally, once we've established all that context, we'll look at few of my favorite future-orienteering activities you can use to sort your next steps in the here and now. Ole' timey dowsing rods are strictly optional.

The Costs of Changing Direction

While plotting a course for your life is more than just the world of choosing a profession, it is one of the biggest decisions we get to make.

In high school, we are forced to put our chips down on a bet for what we want to do with our lives. Will you go to college and if so, how good a college do you aspire to attend? Will you enter the trades and will you need to get a degree for that too? Off to the military? What's your plan, kid? Make a choice already!

My experience boiled down to: "you get no fun electives." College prep somehow meant trigonometry, typing classes, physics and the like. I had other college-bound friends taking golf. For credit.

The good news is that you can always change direction. The bad news is that changing direction will come with a cost.

The size of the cost is what you'll want to consider prior to making the move. Let's explore some of those switching costs.

Literal costs: I'd bet you already have your eye on this one. These are the dollars and cents tied to the change you're considering. That could be a result of expenses involved, lost earnings, or potential costs associated with opportunities for earning you'll miss out on due to the change.

Time: For you to get to where you want to go in life, will the switch mean that you will be adding a bunch of extra years before you'll be able to get there?

Emotion: What will the change bring about to the way you feel day to day? Lots of relief? Stress? Joy? Fear? Grief? If you can guess what the emotional impact of the change will be, you're also giving yourself a window in on other potential literal costs that could be a few dominos further down the chain of change--emotional spending, anyone?

Experience: How will making the move (or choosing to stay) benefit your accumulated experience? Will you add new skills to your portfolio, or does having a shorter or longer tenure help or hurt?

Sunk costs: Here we have a cost that you're better off ignoring. Your brain might tell you that because you've already spent X amount of dollars or Y amount of time doing what you're already doing that it would be a waste of that money or time to change directions. It's a trap! That money is gone. That time is already used up. Stay focused on the potential future costs as described above.

Let's look at some examples of changing directions and what the costs might be for each.

An undergrad changing majors at the end of their junior year

- Literal costs: How many of the credits already earned will be able to be applied to the new major? If the answer is just the general ed ones, this will add many more thousands of dollars to earn that bachelor's.
- Time: Same thing here - this could easily mean adding another year or more of time to complete the degree.
- Emotion: This could fuel student-loan-based anxiety but meanwhile if the new major is a better fit, the change could bring a flood of relief, a sense of belonging, and fulfillment.
- Experience: Even if the credits don't transfer, the knowledge gained will and may lend valuable extra perspective that peers wouldn't have.

A young married couple moving away from family for a career opportunity

- Literal costs: The career opportunity part could mean an increase in income. The moving part comes with costs like renting a moving van, security deposits and first months' rent or the downpayment to buy a new home, if there are kids and family helped with child care, that will become a new expense.
- Time: If staying back home means staying in a depressed job market, where opportunities are less likely to present themselves, moving is a bit like time travel, saving months or years' worth of waiting around. Meanwhile, the new environs will make everything just a little more time-consuming because now every errand begins with a Google search to find the nearest X, Y, or Z.
- Emotion: This would depend a bunch on how close the young couple is with their family and how they feel about

where they will be moving. It also likely means moving away from friends, so loneliness is a risk.

- Experience: Beyond what it would add career-wise, if they've never done something like this, it creates the opportunity to build up a sense of self-reliance.

A 45-year old quitting a job they hate, without another job lined up

- Literal costs: Given that they are quitting without a safety net of another job already set, how many weeks or months of being jobless can they afford? Will switching jobs mean having to accept a lower salary, or will they be able to leverage their decades of experience into a better position?
- Time: Mixed bag here. Finding a job takes a lot of time, and depending on how many resumes they burn through and how many interviews they do or do not get, time can seem to elongate. But being outside of the regimented workday can also provide a greater sense of freedom.
- Emotion: Likely some trepidation of taking the plunge without that job, maybe a shift or loss of identity depending on how long they'd been in the job, but otherwise, goo gobs of relief to get away from a soul-sucking situation.
- Experience: Leaving a job means you get to take the skills you gained, you can list the time served on a resume, and perhaps a good reference from a supervisor or peer. Bad news in this situation, a hated job also likely means you're leaving with anything from a little baggage to full-blown workplace trauma.

As these examples illustrate, making a change can benefit you in one category while it harms you in another. No part of your life exists in isolation. But notice that while it is all connected, choosing to stay or go isn't about right and wrong. It's costs and benefits, pros and cons.

So when you're weighing a big decision, do your best to put away the question "Is this the right thing to do?" Weigh out the costs and decide if you're willing to pay them.

When Your Money is Your Life

I remember conversations with friends and my parents about what kind of career paths to choose where the average salary of the profession was a major talking point but I don't remember us having many (any?) conversations about the gajillion other factors that are also in mix.

How much do you like school and how much schooling (and debt?) might it take to enter one career or another? How many hours a week do you want to give over to your profession? How important is it that you enjoy your work? Or that you can leave work at work and not spend your time at home still thinking about your job? Or for that matter will your work be a Monday to Friday 9-to-5 type of job, allowing you to see friends and family on the nights and weekends? Or will it be a third shift situation or like many doctors, fireman and paramedics where you're working round the clock-ish for days at a time and then off for days at a time?

Perhaps we never had those discussions because the average 18 year old hasn't a clue how to answer most all of those questions. Especially as it relates to what you want your work life to look like. For me, at that point, I only knew what it was like to mow lawns for neighbors and to work at a movie theater. I wouldn't have understood the concept of bringing work home other than the amazing perk of being able to bring home a (clean) garbage bag full of slightly stale popcorn at the end of the night.

What lifestyle do you aspire to and how much money will that require? Kids? How many? Trips abroad for vacation three times a year? Other hobbies that cost money and time? Will you dress to impress and spend the requisite money and time to support that?

These kinds of questions make me think of Vicki Robbins's *Your Money or Your Life*. She has us consider how much of our lives we need to spend in exchange for the things we want by making us look at the math.

For example, if you make $15 an hour and then back out your expenses tied to that wage (taxes, social security, your commute, a wardrobe you need to maintain for the job, etc.) you're left with a new smaller number. Let's say in this case that you have $10 left over to keep our math easy.

Say you want to go out for dinner and a movie. Let's put that at $50 all in. That means you'll have to spend 5 hours working to offset that cost ($50 divided by $10/hour). Is that math mathing for you? Does that sound like a reasonable exchange of your time for your entertainment? 5 hours of working for 3-4 hours of entertainment and a square meal?

Things get more dramatic when we're talking about bigger ticket expenses. Let's go to the biggest ticket that most of us will consider: buying a house.

When Megan and I bought our first house, we had a combined net income of maybe $60,000, after paycheck withholdings. Breaking it down, say I represented half of that number, so $30,000. Divide that by 52 to get $577 a week. Divided by a 40 hour workweek and we get $14.40 per hour of net income. Ope, did I mention that I was actually working 50-ish hours a week? Let's re-do that math. That makes it $11.54 per hour net income. Shoot, I wasn't counting my commute. One hour round trip a day, five days a week. 55 hours. $10.49/hour.

So at that time in my life, I was exchanging an hour of my life to get $10.49 back in my pocket.

So Megan and I start the house hunt process. We meet with our bank, and we get approved up to a $300,000 mortgage. Did I mention it was the spring of 2008? We knew that we'd be foolish to go that high. We bought a lovely home, only a couple years old, for $179,000.

My half of that is $89,500 if we paid cash. We didn't. So that means with interest on a 30-year mortgage, the actual price tag for my half would be about $175,000.

Now if we divide that number by $10.49, we get 16,683 hours. Oof.

$30,000 salary ÷ 52 weeks
= $577 weekly salary
$577 ÷ ~~40 hours~~
~~50 hours~~
55 hours
= $10.49 / hour

Math of real hourly wage

But keep in mind, I couldn't possibly give my whole paycheck over for housing. There's food, utilities, clothing, entertainment, etc. If we use the standard logic of not exceeding 25 percent of your paycheck for housing, that means I'd actually need to divide not by $10.49 but by 25 percent of that: $2.62.

$175,000 divided by $2.62 = 66,794 hours! That's 8,349 workdays = 1,670 weeks = 32 years. Of working. To pay off a first home's 30 year mortgage. At 2008 prices. Oh and by the by, had we gone all the way up to the amount the bank approved us for, it would have required 55 years of work.

Sure sure, there was a good chance that both of us would earn pay raises along the way, allowing for extra payments if we wanted. But that's not the point of this story.

$179,000 home + 30 years of interest
= $350,000 ÷ 2
= my portion: $175,000

$175,000 ÷ ~~$10.49~~ / hour
$2.62 / hour
= 66,794 hours

66,794 hours ÷ 8 hours
= 8,349 work days ÷ 5 day work weeks
= 1,670 weeks ÷ 52 weeks
= 32 years of my life

Math on the home purchase

Your lifestyle—how you eat, dress, spend your time off work, where you live, whether you have kids and what lifestyle you afford them—those are all choices you make along the way, and they all have a price tag, and unless you are a trust fund kid whose life wealth was already figured out for you, that means that you'll have to exchange days, weeks, and years of your life working in order to pay for them.

It all hangs in a balance.

Choose a less luxurious lifestyle and that means you have more flexibility choosing a career path where a big paycheck isn't the most important part of your decision. Or perhaps you want to get to retirement as quickly as possible, so you angle for low cost of living plus as high a salary as you can get, regardless of how much you enjoy the job, because it's about getting to that beach lifestyle by your late 30s!

"Choose a ______ lifestyle" makes it sound like that's a one-time decision. But of course, it isn't. It's a steady accumulation of choices that nets you that luxurious or humble lifestyle. And there's a tricky mechanism in our brains that will catch you when you're not looking.

Scott Galloway, in *The Algebra of Wealth*, cautions those of us looking to build wealth across our lifetime, to beware the slip sliding scale of lifestyle creep. This is the idea that once you have grown accustomed to a type of luxury, it becomes very difficult to move back to your previous humbler ways.

"Luxury" is in the eye of the beholder. It's completely relative based on your taste and experience. Let's look at hotels as an example.

Maybe you've stayed in a Holiday Inn Express before? Would you consider it luxurious? What if all you'd experienced previously was run-down budget hotels? Staying in a place that's clean, kept up, safe, and serves a hot breakfast all might officially qualify as a luxury!

Now picture an A-list celebrity who's been raking in millions of dollars year after year. Do you think they would view staying at a Holiday Inn Express as a luxurious experience? I didn't poll any A-listers to write this chapter, but I think it's a safe bet it would be a solid nope.

Not only is it relative from person to person, but it's also not a fixed property in our own individual minds. This is where Galloway was pointed.

Just like those imagined celebrities who have become accustomed to a very swanky way of life, each little upgrade that you make along the path of your life becomes the new norm to you. And your cost of living goes up accordingly.

That's the steady accumulation of choices I was referring to.

Five years ago, Megan convinced me to go to the salon she frequents to get my hair cut. Previously, I'd been accustomed to going to places like Bo-Rics or SuperCuts. The sort of place that advertises their low-low prices. No shampoo necessary, just hose your client down with a spray bottle like a naughty pet.

Contrast that experience with Megan's salon, where I'm offered some cucumber water while I wait and not only do I get a proper shampoo rather than the spray bottle treatment, the stylist gives me a scalp massage. Bye bye Bo-Rics!

But that comes at a cost. Four times the cost. And I happily pay it, even knowing that I could go back and save money if I wanted. I don't want. I've learned that there's a better way for me to get my hair cut and I no longer dread the process.

That's one choice among many and they all add up.

Can you spot places in your life where you've made some upgrades? Maybe even upgrades upon upgrades upon upgrades? Perhaps in the way you eat, dress, travel, or entertain yourself? Do you have a sense lasting value and gratitude for the upgrade, like me every time I get my scalp massage at the salon?

Two other things to consider:

1. **Beware emotional spending.** If you feel an impulse to go shopping, take a moment to reflect on what you're feeling. Are you bored? Anxious? Celebratory? Angry? Your impulse to buy something won't address the root cause, only distract you with a fleeting dopamine hit. Better to observe your reflex and see what you can learn about yourself rather than throwing away some money on something you don't really need.
2. **Take stock and change what you need to.** Make it a habit to review your habits around money at least once a year, or better yet get yourself an app that helps you keep track

of how you're doing on saving, investing, and spending. Kill those unused subscriptions that bleed money from your accounts. Make sure that your choices support your bigger picture of where you want to get to and by when.

You Are Here

Let's recap. You likely grew up with some ideas about what you wanted to do in life, and if you're like most people, you've changed your mind since then. We've talked about the potential consequences of future changes in direction and how the choices you make with your money and how you spend your time are inseparable.

Now I want you to take everything you've learned and create yourself as clear a picture as you can for what your future is going to look like.

If you've been answering the questions I've asked along the way, you have been preparing for this moment, much like an artist setting out all of their pencils, markers, and brushes as they settle in before a big blank canvas or sheet of paper.

Speaking of which, get yourself a blank sheet of paper and your writing utensil of choice. We have two more activities that you're going to do to help you develop that picture.

First, I'm going to ask you to write your own eulogy, which is a way to get you to zoom way way out on the whole of your life. It will help you capture details that some of these specific questions that I've asked you would miss. They were specific. This activity is wide-open exploration.

Once you've done that, you'll take everything you've written and thought about and boil it down to a short description of what you want your life to be about—this is your Moonshot.

When you capture a beautiful dream for your life that you fall head over heels in love with, you will rearrange your day-to-day, year-to-year life to reach that dream. That includes making changes that might be a little uncomfy for your today-self but contribute in a big way to seeing that dream come true for you.

Remember that bit I shared in chapter 11 about going to the doctor and dentist for the first time in fifteen years as a result of starting to do visioning work? Yeah, like that! Super-uncomfy for Today Jeremy but such a big payoff for Future Me.

A 30,000 Foot View of Your Life

So yeah, that next activity is a big one. The Eulogy.

If the idea of your eventual death is just too scary or difficult to think through, there's also the option of telling your life story. Regardless, it's about getting that big 'ole zoom-out.

This is a completely open-ended activity. You're not being asked any individual questions or pointed down any particular angles of viewing your life.

The thing I appreciate about this activity, beyond its open-ended nature, is that by situating the view from the end of your life, it means that there's nothing more to be done. You've completed your assignment here on Earth and it's purely about looking back at what happened and what it meant for you and your loved ones.

A eulogy, by its nature, is focused on the people who meant the most to you and the ways you spent your time that were the most important and most characteristic of you.

It's unlikely to describe each and every vacation you ever went on, lovely as they all might have been—but it might talk about the trip you took that changed the way you looked at life. It isn't concerned about the busyness of daily life—no mention of running errands or the last TV show you watched. It tells your story. Who you were and why you were loved. Who you loved. How you made a difference during your time here.

The first time I did the Eulogy activity I came away with a revelation that changed the way I was approaching my life at the time. While I was already clear that I wanted to live my life in a way that supported the people around me in building lives they love, and that I had some big ambitions for how to spend my time, and how Megan and I would travel and where we would retire, the thing that actually got me was thinking through who would deliver my eulogy.

I chose my younger brother, Jonathan as the person to deliver it, as well as Megan being in the front row grieving alongside her sister and other family members—a little nod to the universe to not for a second think of taking Megan or Jon before me. When I started composing the words that I wanted Jon to say about me and our relationship, I got zapped by an epiphany: I don't know that I've earned these words from my brother yet. I don't know that we're close enough in our relationship to elicit these words. It changed the way I interacted with Jon when we spoke on the phone or said goodbye after a visit, with me being sure to let him know that I loved him. It's such a small thing, but I will forever be grateful to this activity for providing me with that clarity and sparking that change.

I know that people can struggle with this activity. It can be uncomfortable to be reminded that we only have so much time available to us in this life. Whether you choose to write your eulogy or the story of your life—even if you choose to leave out the actual end of your life in what you write—you're still writing about this finite collection of years that you get to spend (hopefully doing what you love most!).

If that feels like something that could get in your way from doing this activity, I hope I can get you to reconsider. There is nothing that you can do about the whole human mortality thing. It's a package deal. You get some time on this earth to put to use, but you have an expiration date. So, no sense worrying about the fact that it will happen some day and some way for you. You can't control that. This activity is about pulling into focus what you can control.

Another common roadblock people encounter when writing their eulogy is the it-makes-me-uncomfy-to-write-words-for-other-people-to-say-and-way-worse-to-have-them-be-nice-words-about-me thing. I get it. It feels like bragging. But not only bragging, more like mind-controlling a family member or friend and then having them do your bragging for you.

I have a reframe for you to consider: You're not bragging. You're making a promise to the people in your life. The words that you write for them to say—about who you were, what you meant to them, and the things you did that defined your life—that's a plan that you need to execute on. Like the epiphany I had about my relationship with my brother, what will you need to do, between now and that unknown moment, to earn those words?

A Moonshot in the Rough

Once you've captured the big-picture-broad-stroke version of what your future life will look like, the final thing I'm going to ask you to do is to find a way to boil it down to a few sentences-worth of words.

The value of boiling down a vision for you life into a Moonshot is being able to easily share it, which is super-valuable, as I described in the Power of Sharing in chapter 11.

A Moonshot statement is a concise way of expressing what you want your life to be about or what you want it to build toward.

A Moonshot statement might be in the style of accomplishing

something nearly unbelievable, like a personal BHAG (Big Hairy Audacious Goal), as described by Jim Collins in *Good to Great*: "a huge and daunting goal—like a big mountain to climb."

Mike McFall, BIGGBY co-founder and co-author of *The Moonshot Guidebook*, deserves the credit for establishing the practice of finding your Moonshot inside of BIGGBY culture, having developed his own BHAG-style Moonshot years before he and Laura wrote The BIGGBY Freestyle Visioning Tool: to own the Detroit Red Wings.

Having grown up in Milford, Michigan, a town situated just outside the Detroit Metro area and a 45-minute drive from the Joe Louis Arena, then-home of the Red Wings, Mike has a long history and deep emotional connection to the team. It's a near-impossible big goal, and one that stokes the fire in Mike's belly to see personal success as well as the success of the company he co-founded.

A BHAG-style Moonshot has a defined finish line—you will know for sure whether you have accomplished it, and it will also be relatively easy to gauge your progress toward it. I'm not sure what kind of a price tag a NHL team has on it, but I'm certain that Mike does.

The other style of Moonshot statement has no finish line. Rather than being about your life building toward some great accomplishment, it's more about a way of being...like getting your life to a place where you get to live your perfect day every day all while being at your very best as a person.

My Moonshot has elements of each in its current iteration (I'm on my eleventh iteration—more on that in a bit): "To laugh at home every day. To follow my curiosity, keep creating, connecting, and sharing; touching the lives of millions through my work."

The first sentence-and-a-half sum up how I want to live my life. I want a happy home life. That means that no matter what ever other accomplishment that I might chase after, that I'm not willing to sacrifice what Megan and I have built together to achieve it. I want to live in a way that allows me to continue learning and growing and creating things like books and games, but also to be able to share what I've learned with the people around me—that the things I learn aren't just for my own personal benefit, but that its of greater use to the people around me or in my broader community.

The final half-sentence ("—touching the lives of millions through my work") is the part I have fussed with the most while iterating on my Moonshot. No matter the exact words I've used, it's always revolved around the idea that I want my work to make a difference for people.

This is why I think it's important to get a V.1 of your Moonshot down, even if you can feel it isn't 100 percent right. You'll have the opportunity, as you live life, to have your current Moonshot iteration pulling you forward in the direction of your dreams, giving you all the brain-science-y benefits I've described, and then when it's time to sit back down again and take a look at what you've written, you'll have the chance to keep refining, keep polishing, until you've shined up a diamond of a Moonshot statement.

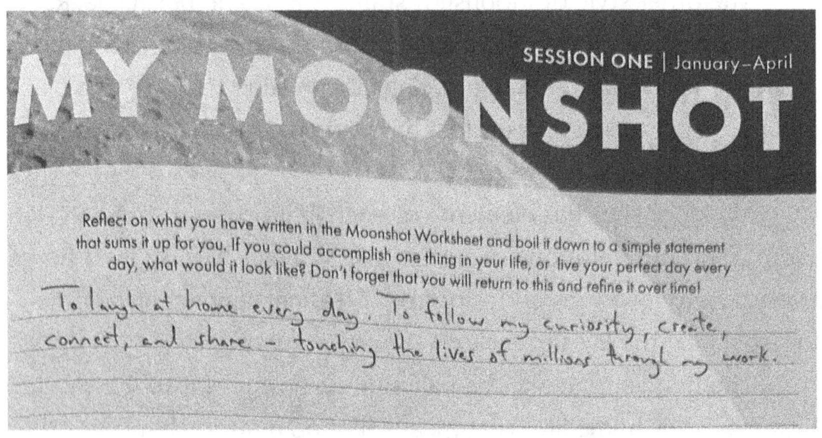

SESSION ONE | January–April
MY MOONSHOT
Reflect on what you have written in the Moonshot Worksheet and boil it down to a simple statement that sums it up for you. If you could accomplish one thing in your life, or live your perfect day every day, what would it look like? Don't forget that you will return to this and refine it over time!
To laugh at home every day. To follow my curiosity, create, connect, and share – touching the lives of millions through my work.

My moonshot statement, January 2024

Get in Motion: Your Eulogy and Moonshot

If you've been putting in the work at the end of each of these chapters by doing the Get In Motion activities, you have churned up enough ideas to be able to capture your eulogy (or life story!) and the first iteration of your Moonshot! So, grab your notebook and get writing!

The Eulogy/Life Story

The important thing is to get that thirty-thousand-foot view of your life. If you write your eulogy, go the extra step and describe the setting, the people who are in attendance, and who will read your eulogy.

Your Moonshot!

Remember, I think of this as a process of refinement across years – you're not carving this into stone, just writing it down for a first version. Scratch-outs are okay! You'll know that you're on the right track if it makes you feel equal parts excited, sparkly, and intimidated.

Bonus points if you grab someone in your life and share this first version with them. Exponential bonus points for each additional person after the first!

The main thing is that you have it, and that means you have a compass that will help you make big decisions in your life. And if you keep returning to it, setting goals around it and sharing, all that beautiful brain science stuff (and/or if you prefer, the Universe or some other higher power) will start to kick in and you will feel the momentum start to build!

Good luck and get writing!

Closing

Bleary-Eyed and Stumbling Forth

I hope I am never judged for my first few moments awake each morning. Megan, I suppose, would have the best opportunity, and so long as there's not some unforeseen breach of privacy headed my direction, the list of people who have that chance is pretty short.

Perhaps in reading this book, you've formed an opinion of me being a sprinting-out-of-the-bed-go-getter, all carpe diem, and so forth.

While I am indeed a morning person (thanks entirely to a few years of 4:30am alarms to get BIGGBY Store #3 open on time), you gotta give me a few minutes to get myself revved up.

These days, whether waking to an alarm or not, my eyes pry open; I take a second to remember what day it is; and then roll myself out of bed. From there, it's all creaks and popping joints, taking uneven Walking Dead steps toward my toothbrush. Systems are coming online. Damage assessment pending. Exercise, a shower, some coffee, and I'll finally feel like a fully-functioning version of myself.

Those first steps after waking are not pretty. I'm sure I look like the 80-year-old version of myself. But it gets the job done. It gets me going until the more pulled-together version of me is ready to take over the reins.

And that's what I hope for you, if you've spent some number of years being swept forward by the momentum of life, just following along in the part that your scripts dictated you play. I hope I've given you an opportunity to wake up and take some stumbling steps forward, living a good and happy life and perhaps when you're ready, living each of your days in way that helps you to intentionally build a life you love.

I'm just so very happy that you are here with me, reading these words. My final advice for you (at least for now):

Keep exploring! No matter where you are in your journey of self-discovery and building your self-awareness, there will always be new revelations. Read everything and watch YouTube videos to uncover things that you didn't know that you didn't know. Get feedback from people in your life and find some blind spots so you can work on those behaviors. If you can afford it and want to do some real digging, get yourself a therapist who you like and trust.

Be kind to yourself! Maybe you don't need this kind of advice. If that is the case, bless you, that's great. But otherwise, if you too have an inner bully, I want you to start practicing being nice to yourself. If you have mean thoughts that recur when you look in the mirror or make a mistake or whatever, it's time to find a replacement—find a phrase that's empowering and say it back to your bully every time they get lippy with you. And if you're ready to get squirmy with it, write down a few affirmations and work it into your daily routine somewhere to say them out loud to yourself. It's just one small way you can rewrite parts of your script in a way that will make you more confident and powerful across time!

Start visioning! Regardless of what method you choose (vision boards, journaling, *The Moonshot Guidebook*, or some other tool), get moving. Among all the different things I've talked about in this book, nothing has made me feel more powerful and more in control of my future than having a visioning practice. Plus, it's just flat-out fun. Find yourself a place and a space in your life where doing that kind of dreaming just feels great. Find a spot that just feels good to sit back and think (your place) at a time where you'll feel best able to do that kind of work (your space).

Just remember, wherever you are in your journey through life, you are whole and perfect.

That doesn't mean that you can't find all kinds of opportunities to grow and make changes in your life and do cool new things with your time. It means you are the only you that you have. Embrace your youness and build a life you will love!

In a spirit of love and opportunity,
Jeremy
April 16, 2023

Acknowledgements

Megan, I love you so much. I'm a better man because you're in my life. Thank you for being my first reader, for the notes you gave, for laughing at my jokes, and for being gracious and letting me share these pieces of our life with my readers.

Dad and Shirley, thank you for your always-on love for Megan and me and the rest of the family. We're all very fortunate to have you as role models. Dad, talking through this book with you chapter-by-chapter as I wrote was really special for me. I love you both.

Mom, you're not here to read this, but I'm glad I'd already started this project while you were still with us and that I was able to share the first few chapters with you. I miss you. Readers, any time I veered off into something funny with an absurdist bent (Accountability Gnome, anyone?), that was me channeling Mom.

Jonathan DeRuiter, I'm so proud of you and the life that you're building. You've been a role model to me in the way that you've thrown yourself into learning and investing in the hobbies you love. Your way of being was an epiphany to me in those years where I was working too much and not fully living. And Melissa Rutherfoord, I'm so glad you're a part of my family. You were a huge comfort to Megan and me in the months of Mom's illness and passing. We love you both.

Nikki Robertson, my copy editor. Nikki, I was so pleased to get to work with you on another book. Dear readers, if you at all enjoyed reading this book, you should send some praise Nikki's way. She helped me cut out funny yet time-consuming wanderings and a few painfully dull stretches!

Bob Fish and Mike McFall, thank you for every chance you've given me. I'm forever grateful for the journey we began ten years ago with Conscious Capitalism, the Forums, our purpose, and shortly thereafter, Boost. You changed my world, again and again, for the better. And Mike, a special thank you for the notes on those early chapters--the critiques made the work better and the praise was wind in my sails.

Tony DiPietro, thank you for all the ways you've challenged me and supported me over the years as well as for all of your kind words and support throughout writing this book. Love you, brother.

To my LifeLab family—Alisha Beck, Ashley Thomas, Brie Roper, Denise Urbain, and Laura Eich—I love you weirdos. Thanks for creating the safe space for me to go to work on myself and for all of the feedback and love along the way.

Stephanie Schlichter, we were a dynamic duo, and I'm so glad we had the opportunity to make each other sharper and stronger in our day to day work because of the trust we'd built.

Nathan Havey, you've left an indelible mark on BIGGBY and on my life. No one makes me dream bigger than you and no one in my life does a better job of creating opportunities for people to change the world. Thank you for the endless inspiration and your friendship.

Mike Srodes and Jim Jenson, I'm so glad that we got the chance to work with you both and for the stamp you've put onto our world through what you taught us and the space you created for us to learn and grow into. I'm grateful for the friendship we developed across those years.

To the rest of my family—Amy, Brandon, Danielle, Dave, Ken, Margaret, Mimi, Bob, Georgette, Diane, Greg, Heidi, Mitzi, Anna, Carson, Leul, Marie, and Morgan—I love you all so much. I feel guilty not giving you each your own individual acknowledgement because you are all special to me and part of my story, but just not directly a part of this particular book. Thank you for all the love and lessons that you've shared with me over the years. I'm grateful for you and I love you.

Similarly, there are so many other friends and mentors who have had a huge influence on me and given me so much love, so many lessons, and countless laughs. Dee, Abbie, Dre, Kristina, Matti, Nathan, Paulie, Sara, Stef, Katie Baker, Kate, Zach, Geoff, Monica, Austin, Becca, Beth, Brooke, Caitlin, Caitlin, Chels and Teej, Collins, Ed, Erica, HP, Ian, Jeannie, Karen, Marilynn, Jodi, John, JSB, Kotia, Kristie, Michelle, Nicole, Nicole, Nikki, Terese, Kevin, Rhoda, Eric, Jane, Joe, Joey, Keegan, Deb, Mohamed, Tim, Tim, Sue, Adam, Bob, Denise, Jon, Kip, Mark, Paula, Randy, Shanna, Chris, Joe, MaryAnne, Mo, Peggy, Richard, Yul, Alex, Kyle, Meghan, Mike, Morgan, Shelley, Dharmesh, Matt, Tom, Tara, Al, Charles, Diane, Julie, Linda, Dan, Karmen, Katie, Mandy, Norma, Rob, Samantha, and Sarah.

Oh, and can't forget Eff, Iz, and Eliza. Love you pups. Megan, you'll have to let them know about their shoutout. Ler u.

Notes

Page 10: Energy consumption of the brain

Rock, D. (2009). Your brain at work: Strategies for overcoming distraction, regaining focus, and working smarter all day long. Harper Business.

Masicampo, E. J., & Baumeister, R. F. (2008). Toward a physiology of dual-process reasoning and judgment: Lemonade, willpower, and expensive rule-based analysis. *Psychological Science*, 19(3), 255–260. https://doi.org/10.1111/j.1467-9280.2008.02077.x

Gailliot, M. T., Baumeister, R. F., DeWall, C. N., Maner, J. K., Plant, E. A., Tice, D. M., Brewer, L. E., & Schmeichel, B. J. (2007). Self-control relies on glucose as a limited energy source: Willpower is more than a metaphor. *Journal of Personality and Social Psychology*, 92(2), 325–336. https://doi.org/10.1037/0022-3514.92.2.325

Page 10: Willpower, an expendable resource

Muraven, M., & Baumeister, R. F. (2000). Self-regulation and depletion of limited resources: Does self-control resemble a muscle? *Psychological Bulletin*, 126(2), 247–259. https://doi.org/10.1037/0033-2909.126.2.247

Baumeister, R. F., Bratslavsky, E., Muraven, M., & Tice, D. M. (1998). Ego depletion: Is the active self a limited resource? *Journal of Personality and Social Psychology*, 74(5), 1252–1265. https://doi.org/10.1037/0022-3514.74.5.1252

Inzlicht, M., & Gutsell, J. N. (2007). Running on empty: Neural signals for self-control failure. *Psychological Science*, 18(11), 933–937. https://doi.org/10.1111/j.1467-9280.2007.02004.x

Job, V., Dweck, C. S., & Walton, G. M. (2010). Ego depletion—Is it all in your head? Implicit theories about willpower affect self-regulation. *Psychological Science*, 21(11), 1686–1693. https://doi.org/10.117

Page 25: Supervisors over-relying on strengths, diminishing their team, know-it-all

Wiseman, L. (2010). *Multipliers: How the best leaders make everyone smarter.* Harper Business.

Page 39: Signs of self-limiting beliefs

Sincero, J. (2013). *You are a badass: How to stop doubting your greatness and start living an awesome life.* Running Press.

Page 42: We're all the hero of our own story

Maguire, G. (1995). *Wicked: The life and times of the wicked witch of the West.* HarperCollins.

Covey, S. R. (1989). *The 7 habits of highly effective people: Powerful lessons in personal change.* Free Press.

Notes

Page 47: People are hard to hate up close
Brown, B. (2017). *Braving the wilderness: The quest for true belonging and the courage to stand alone.* Random House.

Pages 71, 172: Personality tests, common language
Gallup. (2007). *StrengthsFinder 2.0.* Gallup Press.

Page 139: Visioning and me, Primary Aim
Gerber, M. E. (1995). *The E-myth revisited: Why most small businesses don't work and what to do about it.* Harper Business.

Page 142: *The Moonshot Guidebook*
McFall, M. J., Eich, L., & DeRuiter, J. (2020). *The moonshot guidebook: A step-by-step approach to make your big ideas a reality.* Conscious Capitalism Press.

Page 156: Placebos and nocebos
Crawford, L. S., Mills, E. P., Hanson, T., Macey, P. M., Glarin, R., Macefield, V. G., Keay, K. A., & Henderson, L. A. (2021). Brainstem mechanisms of pain modulation: A within-subjects 7T fMRI study of placebo analgesic and nocebo hyperalgesic responses. *Journal of Neuroscience*, 41(47), 9794–9806. https://doi.org/10.1523/JNEUROSCI.0806-21.2021

Page 162: Visualization
University of Colorado at Boulder. (2018, December 10). Your brain on imagination: It's a lot like reality, study shows. *ScienceDaily.* https://www.sciencedaily.com/releases/2018/12/181210144943.htm

Page 164: Reticular activating system
Hyde, J., & Garcia-Rill, E. (2015). Ascending projections of the RAS. In E. Garcia-Rill (Ed.), *Waking and the reticular activating system in health and disease* (pp. 107–128). Academic Press.

Page 164: Visualization
Murphy, S., Jowdy, D., & Durtschi, S. (1990). Report on the US Olympic Committee survey on imagery use in sport. Colorado Springs, CO: US OlympicTraining Center.

Page 181: Empathy and sympathy
Brown, B. (2018). *Dare to lead: Brave work. Tough conversations. Whole hearts.* Random House.

Page 193: Welcome to the 94%
Universidad Carlos III de Madrid - Oficina de Información Científica. (2014, November 10). Only 6% of people work in the occupations they aspired to in childhood. *ScienceDaily.* https://www.sciencedaily.com/releases/2014/11/141110084110.htm

Page 198: Exchanging your time for a paycheck
Robbins, V., & Dominguez, J. (2008). *Your money or your life: 9 steps to transforming your*

relationship with money and achieving financial independence. Penguin Books.

Page 201: Lifestyle creep

Galloway, S. (2020). *The algebra of wealth: A simple formula for financial security*. Portfolio.

Page 208: Big hairy audacious goal

Collins, J. (2001). *Good to great: Why some companies make the leap... and others don't*. Harper Business.

Index

7 Habits of Highly Effective People, The, 39, 41

accountability gnome, 140, 141
affirmations
  a methodology, 121
  activity, 130
  as a reflex, 120
  examples, 122, 123
  morning routine, 162, 206
Algebra of Wealth, The, 195
anger, 31, 52, 53, 161
anxiety, 30
argument, 23, 42

Baader-Meinhof phenomenon, 134, 141
barista, 69, 72, 124
Beck, Alisha, 14, 76, 88, 146, 174, 176, 177
beer, 56-58, 100, 107
belief, 34, 35, 80, 152
BHAG, 201
bias, 43, 134
BIGGBY COFFEE, 20, 23, 24, 40, 137
  annual franchise meeting, 75, 76
  coachees, 11, 86, 122
  cultural values, 97
  leadership forums, 13, 14, 99
  loyalty cards, 110
  personal growth because of, 13, 132, 141, 142, 167
  relation to *Moonshot Guidebook*, 201
  ridiculous coworkers, 43
  stores, 70-73, 205
  training, 73, 75, 124, 125
  use of DiSC, 68
blind spot
  creates judgment, 17
  example of, 173, 174, 181, 182
  relationship to strengths 171
  seeing into them 69
  working on them 172

books, 1, 2, 13, 22, 40, 41, 43, 100, 107, 132, 135, 168, 169, 175, 202
BOOST Sphere, 137, 141, 180
Borton, Chelsea, 86
brain
  as a filter, 134, 135, 141, 164
  associative loop, 8
  brain energy, 8, 63
  brain-body connection, 152, 157
  cerebral cortex, 157
  creating meaning, 27-30, 43
  goblins, 55
  good brain chemicals, 116, 162, 163
  habit formation, 8
  prefrontal cortex, 8, 91
  reticular activating system, 159, 160, 163
  sensorimotor loop, 8
  sensory processing, 19
  teenage development, 91, 92
brain science, 8, 134, 139, 151, 157, 202, 203
Braving the Wilderness, 42
Brown, Brené, 42, 175, 176
Brown, David, 111
bully
  bullying, 33, 34, 117
  inner bully, 118, 119, 125, 126

cerebral cortex, (see brain)
children, (see kids)
church, 3, 65, 85, 95, 98
coaching
  coaching program, 11, 43, 53, 57, 58, 87, 122, 137, 142, 173, 174

in sports, 158
peer-to-peer coaching, 23, 24
college 4, 56, 93, 95, 124, 187
Collins, Jim, 201
compliment, 111, 122, 126-128
conscious
awareness, 11, 37, 53, 54, 62, 73, 84, 85, 116, 141, 174
thought, 8, 9, 19, 25, 29, 159
Conscious Capitalism, 138, 142
Covey, Stephen R., 39, 40, 46
COVID, 27, 40, 42, 142
Crux Move Consulting, 14

Dare to Lead, 175
decisions, 8, 9, 19, 43, 118, 180, 187, 191, 194
see also: conscious
DeRuiter, Elaine, 73
DeRuiter, Jerry, 1, 4, 79, 84, 85, 95, 107, 185
DeRuiter, Jonathan, 1, 21, 62, 79, 199
DeRuiter, Megan, 5, 6, 7, 28-30, 37, 40, 44, 50, 52-54, 62, 64, 86, 87, 101, 108, 118, 136, 137, 162, 172, 177, 178, 192, 196, 199, 201, 205
Detroit Red Wings, 201
dials, 83-86, 90
DiPietro, Tony, 20, 23-25, 76
DiSC, 68, 69, 167
dogs, 39, 52, 66, 108, 162, 173
dreaming, 11, 133, 142, 157, 186
dreams, 38, 43, 100, 132, 136, 142, 162, 186
achieving, 121, 149, 164, 198
sharing, 141, 142
writing down, 133, 135, 138, 139, 145, 161, 197
visualizing, 163

Eich, Laura, 14, 138, 142, 150, 154, 180-182, 201
embarrassment, 31, 88
emotion, 9, 23, 27, 53, 63, 63, 77, 164
emotional intelligence, 89
emotional spending, 196
empathy, 14, 92, 174, 175, 177
E-Myth Revisited, The, 135
energy, 9, 67, 75, 134, 155, 156, 163, 173, 181
being yourself, 100, 102
bouncing back, 72, 73
emotional, 62, 63
mental, 62, 63, 70
motivator, 68, 76, 77
physical, 62, 63
resource for the brain, 8, 26
spiritual, 62, 63
stressor, 68, 76, 77
Erck, Matt, 56
eulogy, 197-199, 203
extrovert, 14-16, 68, 70, 75

family, 3, 40, 41, 57, 78, 89, 98, 125, 126, 143, 147, 189-191, 200
my family, 35, 36, 43, 186, 199
feedback, 77, 80, 122, 183, 184, 206
find a replacement, 206
Fish, Bob, 13, 14, 154
Flight Plan, 175
franchise owners, 13, 14, 97
friends, 4, 78, 83, 89, 97, 98, 123, 125, 126, 128, 141, 145, 149, 183, 190
my friends, 5, 7, 21, 40, 43, 85, 87, 94-96, 99, 106, 147, 174, 191

Galloway, Scott, 195
Gallup, 168
Geenan, Jon, 99
Gerber, Michael, 135
Gilkey, John, 86
goblin, 54-59, 140, 141
Good to Great, 201
gratitude, 121, 128, 162, 178, 196
guilt, 30

habits, 11, 22, 55, 121
  bad habits, 51, 55, 56, 123
  good habits, 115, 135, 149, 155, 163, 196
  changing a habit, 26, 55, 123
  replacing conscious thought, 8, 20, 30
Havey, Nathan, 141, 142
Headspace app, 155, 156

identity, 58, 92, 96, 99
imagination, 46, 52
introvert, 14-16, 69, 73, 74
Jenson, Jim, 14-16
Jesus Christ, 134

kids, 39, 79, 98, 132, 163, 185, 186, 194
  being themselves, 91
  bullying, 33, 34
  having kids, 7
  me as a kid, 1, 4, 20, 21, 32-34, 79, 92, 105-107, 185, 186
  relation to the momentum of life, 11, 12
  relation to scripts, 132
Kleist, Margaret, 199

Laninga, Kelli, 14
leadership forums, 14, 99, 135, 180
learning, 13, 15, 19, 43, 68, 119, 145, 168, 202
Ledecky, Katie, 158
Life You Love Laboratory, 51, 86, 121
LifeLab, (see Life You Love Laboratory)
lifestyle, 187, 191, 194
Lunar Landscape, 161

manifesting, 134
marriage, 4, 6, 44, 53
McCobin, Alexander, 142
McFall, Mike, 13, 14, 154, 201
meditation, 121, 151, 154-156, 162
mental imagery, 157, 161, 163
Michigan State University, 5, 69, 93-95
milksteamer, 70, 72, 73
mirror, 11, 51, 80, 112-114, 117-119, 121, 129, 168, 206
momentum of life, 2, 8, 9, 11, 131, 206
Moonshot Guidebook, The, 138, 141, 142, 147, 149, 150, 161, 175, 201, 207
Moonshot statement, 201-203
Mosenzon, Yoram, 51
motivators, 17, 68
Multipliers, 22, 23

nature, 63, 66, 156
nocebo effect, 152
nociception, 159
Nolan, Eric, 70, 71

parents
  independence from, 92, 93, 95
  my parents, 4, 7, 20, 21, 79, 84, 93, 191
  relation to our scripts, 3, 4, 7, 12, 126
passive-aggression, 52
patterns, 19, 20, 27, 29, 30, 52, 55, 120, 126, 144
peace, 63, 66, 77, 178
PERC, 69
perception, 10, 51
personality, 67, 68, 74, 83, 84, 88, 90, 107, 174
personality test, 67, 69, 168, 170
perspective
  diversity of, 23, 94, 169
  earned, 23, 43, 46, 49, 109
  empathy, 92, 169, 170
  getting outside your, 4, 10, 39, 38, 40, 46, 72, 128, 170
  relation to feedback, 80
  relation to opinion, 101
  self-perception, (see self-perception)
Phelps, Michael, 158
placebo effect, 151, 152
presets, 83-86, 89
primary aim, 135, 137
problem-solving, 66, 88, 174

proprioception, 159
purpose, 51, 63, 131, 142
RAS, (see reticular activating system)
reality, 19, 132, 149, 163
  disconnect from, 113, 114, 122,
  reality check, 36, 69
  self-created, 29, 30, 113
religion, 63, 65, 95
resentment, 30
reticular activating system, (see brain)
Robbins, Vicki, 192
Roeder, Candice, 4, 20, 34, 40, 61, 62, 79, 84, 85, 105
Roper, Brie, 14, 57, 65, 67, 64, 76, 138
Rosenberg, Marshall, 51
Rutherfoord, Melissa, 62

Savage, Dan, 98, 103
Schitt's Creek, 88
Schlichter, Stephanie, 14, 169
school
  deciding our future during, 187
  grading system's effect, 168
  and our presets, 84, 85
  and our scripts, 3, 20, 22
script, 3, 4, 6-8, 11, 20, 26, 119, 132, 206
self-awareness, 16, 54, 63, 68, 87, 127, 156, 167, 181-183, 206
self-control, 54
self-deprecating humor, 123-125
self-image, 106
self-limiting beliefs, 34, 107, 119
self-perception, 80, 106, 107, 114
self-talk, 10, 80, 92, 106, 107, 113, 118-120
self-worth, 120
sensory input, 19, 157, 159, 160
shame, 9, 31, 105
Sincero, Jen, 35, 146
social media, 2, 8, 21, 33, 42, 83, 84, 164
spirituality, 63, 65
Srodes, Michael, 14-16
stories
  about our past, 31, 33
  heroes of our own, 37-39, 46
  from bullying, 34
  that limit us, 107
  rewriting them, 35, 36, 46, 47
  that become reality, 29-32, 40
  to empower, 11, 34, 41, 46, 112
strengths
  balanced by others', 23, 25, 68, 169, 170
  cultivating them, 175, 183
  tie to weaknesses, 22, 167, 168, 171
  work styles, 16, 168
Strengthsfinder 2.0, 67, 167-170
stress, 6, 41, 156
stressors, 17, 68, 76, 77
subconscious, 4, 19, 20, 23, 26, 29, 43, 106, 114
support, 13, 14, 25, 53, 54, 62, 95, 125, 180, 183, 192

teacher, 5, 21, 23, 32, 33, 79, 93, 96
team
  becoming stronger, 17, 68, 172
  Detroit Red Wings, 201
  leadership team, 22, 25, 154
  LifeLab team, 17, 51, 86, 138
  operations team, 14, 17
teenagers, 84, 91, 92, 106
Tierney, Caitlin, 86
Tykocki, Nathan, 5

VanderHoff, Brandon, 5
vision
  foggy, 142,
  of the future, 133, 147, 200
  sharing it, 137, 139
  sight, 79
  writing it down, 133, 136, 139, 144
vision board, 139, 145-149, 161, 164, 207
visioning
  and achievement, 138, 139, 142, 175, 201

definition, 133
practice, 135, 142, 145, 148-150, 158, 161
schools of thought, 134
visualization, 121, 151, 156-162
Vonn, Lindsey, 158
vulnerability, 51

willpower, 8, 63
Wiseman, Liz, 22
work styles, 14, 15, 68, 84
workshops, 51, 121, 138, 146
worldview, 3, 37, 43, 49

You Are a Badass, 35, 146
Your Money or Your Life, 192

Also by Jeremy DeRuiter

The Moonshot Guidebook

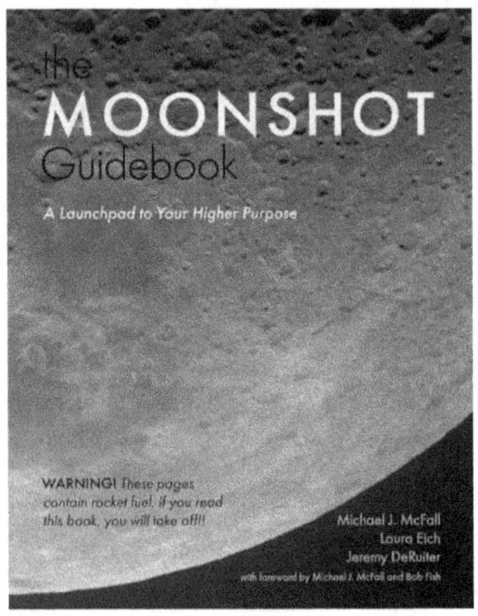

At BIGGBY COFFEE, we believe that knowing who you want to be is a foundational component to building a life you love. *The Moonshot Guidebook*—initially a visioning tool for BIGGBY Home Office employees—will help you to refine a vision for your life by helping you to establish your Moonshot!

www.moonshotguidebook.com

Find Your Moonshot game

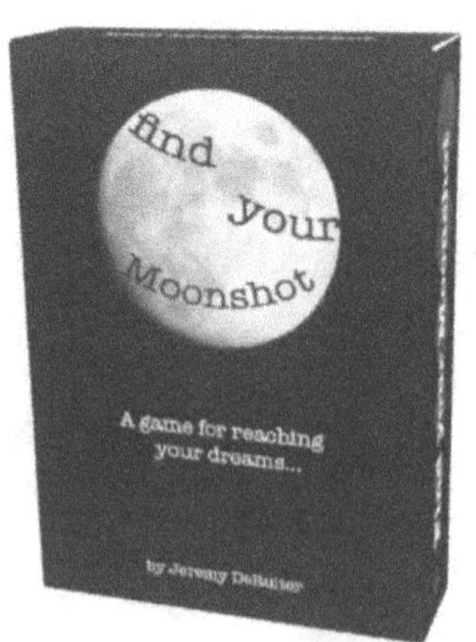

Find Your Moonshot includes more than 200 questions that will help you think through what you want your future to look like and feel like. With six different ways to play, it's an easy and fun way into the practice of visioning, a powerful tool for building a life you love!

www.findyourmoonshot.com

www.ingramcontent.com/pod-product-compliance
Lightning Source LLC
Chambersburg PA
CBHW062051270326
41931CB00013B/3030
* 9 7 9 8 2 1 8 5 2 1 4 1 7 *